The Poems of Robert Dinsmoor

The 'Rustic Bard' of New Hampshire

Introduced by

FRANK FERGUSON
ALISTER McREYNOLDS

ULSTER HISTORICAL FOUNDATION

ACKNOWLEDGEMENT TO THE 2012 EDITION
Ulster Historical Foundation is pleased to acknowledge support for the publication of the first edition of this work provided by the Ulster University.

COVER IMAGE
Overmantel Picture, unknown American artist *c.* 1800
Courtesy of Currier Museum of Art, Manchester, New Hampshire.
Museum Purchase: The Henry Melville Fuller Acquisition Fund, 2004.7

First published as
Robert Dinsmoor's Scotch-Irish Poems on Friends and Family
in 2012 by Ulster Historical Foundation.
This edition 2021.
www.ancestryireland.com
www.booksireland.org.uk

Except as otherwise permitted under the Copyright, Designs and Patents Act 1988, this publication may only be reproduced, stored or transmitted in any form or by any means with the prior permission in writing of the publisher or, in the case of reprographic reproduction, in accordance with the terms of a licence issued by The Copyright Licensing Agency. Enquiries concerning reproduction outside those terms should be sent to the publisher.

© Frank Ferguson and Alister McReynolds
ISBN: 978-1-913993-17-7

Design and formatting by FPM Publishing
Printed by SPRINT-print Ltd

Frank Ferguson is the Research Director for English Language and Literature at Ulster University. He has over twenty years' experience as a researcher and teacher in literary studies. He has written and edited a number of significant texts on Ulster-Scottish and Irish literature. Frank continues to lead a number of ongoing academic and community projects on Irish and Ulster-Scots writing. His research interests include: Ulster and Scottish writing, literary diaspora studies, Scotch-Irish literature and culture, Irish and British book history and the study of the Romantic period ballad in Britain and Ireland.

Alister McReynolds has broad educational experience as a former Further Education Principal. He has written numerous articles and books that focus on the Scotch-Irish in America and is particularly absorbed by their poetry and music and overall contribution to the history and culture of the United States.

He has wide experience of teaching at all levels including a recent popular series of classes at Queen's University Belfast Open Learning which focused on poetry and the work of Bob Dylan. He was awarded an Honorary Fellowship with the Ulster University in 2006.

Alister is married with three grown-up kids and lives in County Antrim.

Contents

List of Poems	vi
Acknowledgements	xii
Introduction	xiii
Title Page To 'Incidental Poems By Robert Dinsmoor'	xxvi
Original Preface	xxvii
Life Of The Author Written By Himself, In A Letter To Silas Betton, Esq. Of Salem, N.H.	xxxii
A Letter From Robert Dinsmore Of Bellywattick, Ireland To John Dinsmore Of Londonderry	xl
The Poems of Robert Dinsmoor Edited by Frank Ferguson	1
Endnotes	196
Glossary	197
Teachers' Notes	205
Afterword (by Alister McReynolds)	210

List of Poems

Skip's Last Advice.	2
An Answer To Dr John Park's Letter, Accompanying A Present Of Burns's "Reliques".	5
To Mrs. Agnes Park, On Receiving From Her A Copy Of "Waverly".	9
To Silas Betton.	11
Silas Betton To Robert Dinsmoor.	12
Robert Dinsmoor To Silas Betton.	14
A Poetical Letter Addressed To Mr. Allen, Printer And Editor Of The Merrimack Intelligencer.	16
Samuel Armor To Robert Dinsmoor.	18
Robert Dinsmoor To Samuel Armor.	20
Lines Addressed To Lt. David Gregg, On The Return Of The Soldiers From Bennington Battle, Sept, 26, 1777.	22
Lines, Wherein Young Jonney Praises His Cousin Molly.	24
Robert Dinsmoor To Silas Betton.	25
The Poet's Farewell To The Muses.	26
Robert Dinsmoor To Silas Betton.	33
Spring's Lamentation And Confession Inscribed To Silas Betton, Esq.	36
Robert Dinsmoor To Silas Betton.	41
The Sparrow.	42
A Father's Lament For The Death Of A Favourite Daughter.	44

THE POEMS: DETAILED CONTENTS

Letter From Robert Dinsmoor To His Daughter.	46
Robert Dinsmoor To His Daughter Sally.	47
Robert Dinsmoor To Silas Betton.	49
The Post-Boy's Address. The Carrier Of The Merrimack Intelligencer To His Patrons. January, 1813.	50
Robert Dinsmoor To Silas Betton.	54
Ninian C. Betton To Silas Betton.	55
Echo To The Bard's Answer.	56
Response To The "Echo".	58
Robert Dinsmoor To Silas Betton.	61
Retrospect After A Fit Of Severe Sickness.	64
Robert Dinsmoor To Peter Ayer.	68
To Miss Harriet Ayer.	69
Peter Ayer To Robert Dinsmoor.	71
The Last Of Bonaparte.	72
Robert Dinsmoor To Silas Betton.	73
Thanksgiving Day.	75
Rev. David M'Gregore To R. Dinsmoor.	78
Answer To The Rev. David M'Gregore.	81
Robert Dinsmoor To Silas Betton.	83
Robert Dinsmoor To Silas Betton.	85
John Nesmith To Robert Dinsmoor.	88
Robert Dinsmoor To Mary E. Dinsmoor.	89
Silas Betton To Robert Dinsmoor.	92
Robert Dinsmoor To Silas Betton, In Answer To The Foregoing Letter.	93

A Farewell To Miss M. E. D., Of Keene, The Bard's Neice, After A Visit To Her Friends In Windham.	96
Robert Dinsmoor To Miss Ann Orr, Of Bedford.	97
Robert Dinsmoor To Henry Davidson.	99
Robert Dinsmoor To Sarah Davidson.	101
A Farewell.	102
A Riddle, Which Appeared In Robert B. Thomas's "Farmer's Alamanac", For The Year, 1807.	104
Answer To The Foregoing.	105
To Dea. S. Whittemore, Salem, Mass.	106
Address To The Branch Church, In Salem, Mass.	107
A Song, By J.N., Teacher Of Music In Windham, 1820.	109
Answer To The "Minstrel Of Nashua".	111
Introduction To "Balaam's Answer".	113
Balaam's Answer.	114
Missionary Hymn – By J.N., "Minstrel".	116
To J.N.	117
To Robert Dinsmoor Titcomb – A Young Namesake.	118
Lines, Written By Joseph Ladd, Merchant Of Belfast, On The Back Of A Dollar Bill, Which He Had Sent To Castine In The Morning, By Way Of Paying A Debt, And It Returned Back To Him In The Evening Of The Same Day, With Twenty More.	120
In The Month Of October, 1820, The Bard Made A Short Visit To His Friends In Belfast, Me., And When He Was Just About To Leave Them, He Wrote The Following Lines In Imitation of Burns, And Left Them With Mr. Ladd, Who Had Treated Him With Much Kindness.	121
Mrs. Elizabeth Hamilton's Compact With Old Age.	122

Address To Mrs. S. G., Of Londonderry,
Accompanying The Foregoing Poem. 125

Verses Addressed To Robert Burns The Airshire Poet. 127

The Bard's Answer To Mr. F. Was Published In Belfast,
In The Following Manner: – "For The Hancock Gazette.
Lines Written By A Gentleman To A Friend In This
Town, After Receiving From Him A Copy Of The "Address
To Robert Burns," Which Was Printed In The Belfast Gazette,
Some Time Since; With A Request That He Would Send Him
"Mrs. Hamilton's Compact With Old Age," Which
Appeared In One Of The Christian Disciples, For The
Last Year". 130

Monody On The Death Of Silas Betton, Esq.,
To Lieut. Pearson Titcomb Of Salem, N.H. 132

Pearson Titcomb To Robert Dinsmoor. 134

Robert Dinsmoor To A Friend, When The Writer
Was Confined With The Palsy, And Hearing Of
Number Of Deaths Among His Friends. 135

The Bard Having Observed In The Gazette And Patriot,
Printed In Haverhill, Of Which He Was A Patron,
The Following Paragraph, It Is Here Inserted As An
Apology For The Answer. 137

Answer To The Call In The Gazette And Patriot. 138

The Author To His Friend, Col. Silas Dinsmoor,
Of Mobile, Alabama. In Scotch, The Dialect Of
Their Ancestors. 139

Antiquity – The Auld Gun. 143

The Following Letter, Is An Answer To I. A. D., The
Bard's Nephew, Who Had Written To Him With A
View To Rectify Some Misunderstanding Between Them. 144

Robert Dinsmoor To John Orr, Esq. Of Bedford,
On Returning Young's Night Thoughts, March 1786. 146

An Ode, Written At the Request Of The Committee Of Arrangements For The Celebration of Independence, Windham, July 4, 1825.	148
A Scrap – Robert Dinsmoor To Dea. Issac Cochran, Of Antrim, N.H., His Mother's Brother, Who Was A Lieut, At The Taking Of Gen. Burgoyne, Oct. 17, 1777. A Short Review Of That Expedition.	150
Ode, Sung At The Dedication Of The New Brick School-House, In Windham.	153
The Braes Of Glenniffer, By Tannahill: Presented By Miss Elizabeth Williams, To The "Rustic Bard".	155
The Braes Of Glenniffer.	156
Robert Dinsmoor To Miss E. Williams, With A Copy Of "Mrs. E. Hamilton's Ain Fireside".	157
My Ain Fireside – By Mrs. Elizabeth Hamilton.	158
To The Editor Of The Haverhill Gazette And Patriot (Poesy On An Old Tea-Pot).	159
Robert Dinsmoor To The Rev. William Miltmore, Falmouth, Maine.	162
Epitaph On Madam Miltimore.	164
The Following Was Sent To Mr. Betton, On Returning To Him Burns's And M'Neil's Poems, Who Had Lent Them To The "Rustic Bard".	165
Answer To Robert Dinsmoor, Presenting Him With Burns, May 8, 1809.	167
Robert Dinsmoor To Silas Betton.	172
Lines Written By A Gentleman For His Wife, On A Work-Bag, With Permanent Ink.	175
By A Special Request From The Same Gentleman And His Lady, The Following Lines Were Written For the Other Side Of The Work-Bag, By The "Rustic Bard".	176

To Issac M'Gaw, Esq. A Young Lawyer And His Wife, Soon After Marriage.	177
To Mr. Isaiah Webster, 2d, Haverhill, Mass., On The Fleeting Nature Of Time – January 1827.	179
Epitaph For The Author's Wife, Who Died June 1, 1799, In The 38th Year Of Her Age.	181
To Miss E.C., At The Close Of Her School, In Windham.	182
To The Editor Of The Haverhill Gazette And Patriot.	183
To Rev. Mr. ———, Of B———.	185
To Catherine Abbot, Preceptress Of Greenland Academy.	186
To Miss Catharine Abbot.	187
To Mrs. Sarah Davidson, The Bard's Daughter, Belfast, Maine.	188
J.G. Whittier To The "Rustic Bard".	190
Robert Dinsmoor To Edward P. Harris, Of Chesterfield.	193
Concluding Verse For "Skip's Last Advice," Received Too Late To Be Incorporated With The Original Piece.	195

Acknowledgements

We are very grateful to a number of people for assisting in the development of this book. Firstly we would thank Fintan Mullan and William Roulston of the Ulster Historical Foundation for their wisdom, support and patience in the bringing to the press of this edition.

We would like to extend our warm gratitude to Professor John Wilson and to Professor Frank Lyons at Ulster University for the financial support they provided for the research and editing of the text. Many thanks are also extended to Mark Thompson for the access he provided to an original copy of the poems.

Special gratitude is given to Carol Baraniuk for her reading of drafts of the introduction and her guidance on the teacher's notes section. Thanks are also offered to Rebecca Graham for her advice on the teacher's notes from an American educationalist's point of view. Appreciation is extended to John and Val Mann, for their ongoing support, friendship and enthusiasm for the reconnection of links across the Atlantic. Deepest gratitude is also given to our wives and families who have put up with many months of discussion and debate about Ulster Scots and Scotch Irish poets.

Ultimately, we feel much thankfulness towards the many descendants of the Dinsmoor/Dinsmore families who contacted us in the course of our editing and research, particularly Brad Dinsmore, who very kindly shared his interest in his ancestor and in the local history of Windham, and it is to this remarkable extended family, past, present and yet to come to whom we dedicate this book.

Introduction

We are all living stories of our family history. In the case of the poet Robert Dinsmoor of Windham, New Hampshire, his remarkable life is an iconic representation of the bravery of countless ancestors as they travelled the perilous route from Scotland to Ireland to America. War, hunger, and the uncertain journey from the Old World to the New might have at any time ended this story before it began.

It is sometimes difficult to work out exactly what makes people move from one place to another. For some the desire for adventure and new surroundings overtakes all other concerns; for others the need for freedom to express themselves as they see fit pushes them to go; yet others follow the belief that they will find the place that will reward them with wealth and an easy life. The longing for a better place is perhaps within all human beings, and this desire was strong within the Dinsmoors. For Robert Dinsmoor's family perhaps all of these reasons motivated their move from Scotland over to Ireland and then to North America in the eighteenth century. And we know this because he left a record of his story in poetry and prose.

In 1828 Robert Dinsmoor, published his only collection, *Incidental Poems*. This book reveals how emigrants can make sense of their European past and American present through writing in a combination of the speech of their former country and the everyday language of the world they experienced when they looked out of their windows in New England.* While it might seem strange to us to have a book of poems that is half written in Scots and English, it was certainly not strange to them. Just as

---

* In this introduction we adopt the older usage of the word 'Scotch' to indicate the people of Scotland and the variety of English spoken by these settlers and their descendants in keeping with the practice of Dinsmoor and his contemporaries.

they learned to negotiate the physical American frontier between the great woods, rivers and lakes they became skilled in navigating between the great worlds of language and literature: between the Old World and New World, and between British and American English, and the rainbow of languages of native Americans and other settlers. To settle the land required energy, guts and determination; and often social niceties were laid aside just to survive. Thus it followed that the literature that was produced was itself also energetic, powerful and focused on the everyday. Like all good folk literature it was earthy, rough textured and given to making fun and enjoying life, while at the same time being aware of the sorrows and difficulties of living. Conversational more than stiffly formal, it was adaptable and knowing, apt to borrow ideas and styles from elsewhere, and like America itself, aware that it was building to a situation from which it would declare its independence.

To many of his readers Dinsmoor was known as the 'Rustic Bard'. However to take Dinsmoor at face value as the 'Rustic Bard', as he was called, is to miss a great deal of his genius as a poet. 'Rustic Bard' might seem a somewhat contradictory name. Bard is a very 'highfalutin' word for a poet, with associations with national significance and prime social importance, who traditionally was viewed as a prophet figure for his or her nation. To suggest Dinsmoor as a 'rustic' bard, i.e. a country or rural poet, proposes that he was the spokesperson for his local area, but one who had only a limited, local appeal, and a rather lower class one at that. We are never sure as readers, then, if we are meant to assume that Dinsmoor is an important local voice for the people, or a sort of comedy act pretending to speak up on community issues. This uncertainty helped Dinsmoor and other poets like him, who could avoid censure of their work by presenting themselves superficially as unsophisticated, comic versifiers. For those in the know, these could be interpreted as highly dangerous political statements, camouflaged as folk poetry. But only those familiar with the language of Scotland, Ulster and the Scotch-Irish of New England, and with the tradition of their poetry could crack the codes and work out what was really being said. To some Dinsmoor might be mistaken as a homely backwoods poet, sharing his faith and humour with the townspeople of Windham and Haverill, New Hamphshire. Closer inspection of his abilities as a poet, his reading of other poets and his political statements suggests a shrewder, more subtle and more complex writer at work.

Dinsmoor's forebears, just like his poems, connect Scotland, Ireland and America. Ancestry and the concept of homeland are of vital importance to Dinsmoor and it would be wrong to think of his book as simply a book of poems. It reads like a classic success story, evidence of a third generation immigrant family who had achieved wealth and power and influence, and some of whose members represented the state as Governor. The book begins with a fascinating narrative of his family history and builds to form a record of his social standing through intermingling throughout the book a series of replications of letters to and from friends and family. It chronicles the Dinsmoors' history in New England and provides a wonderful snapshot of colonial and post colonial New England life with its family gatherings, social events, hardships and sense of community. Moreover this family history, culminating in a number of poems that record significant events and controversies places Robert Dinsmoor and his family at the forefront of public life. This suggests that in reality he was a type of writer who recorded and commentated on major events. This standing is further enhanced when one considers the important role his family played in the politics and public life of New Hampshire: both his brother Samuel (1776–1835), and his nephew, also Samuel Dinsmoor (1799–1869), gained the state governorship.

Dinsmoor Family History

Dinsmoor's family history is as thrilling as an adventure story. His father's great-grandfather, John Dinsmoor, had come to Co. Antrim (in the north of Ireland) from Achenmead near the River Tweed in Scotland following a family dispute with his brother. He subsequently settled at Ballywattick which lies on the Coleraine side of Ballymoney. In the 1720s his son emigrated to America, not long after the exodus of the Rev. McGregor. James McGregor has been described as 'The Moses of the Scotch Irish in America.' He was the Presbyterian Minister in Aghadowey Co. Londonderry and on 4th August 1718, he arrived in Boston with 16 families from his congregation on a brigantine called the Robert. That was the first ship in a flotilla of five which led the way for other Scotch-Irish to come to New England. The reasons for sailing were many; some claimed they left to avoid religious persecution in Ireland; others suggest they went for economic reasons to build a better life in America.

John Dinsmoor junior, who was known in America as 'Daddy Dinsmoor', settled first in Maine at Fort George. There he enjoyed, as he believed, good relations with his Native American neighbours whose tribesmen often repeated to him the mantra, 'All one Brother'. Notwithstanding that however he was kidnapped by them and held in captivity for three months. The tribesmen's chief, also John, befriended him during this period and he eventually set him free, enabling him to make his way to the Scotch-Irish settlement of Londonderry, New Hampshire. Many of the inhabitants of that town knew him and he was granted 100 acres by its proprietors. He was a stonemason by trade and so not surprisingly he built a stone house and sent word back to Ballymoney for his wife and children to join him in the New World. In 1731 his son William was born and William was the father of Robert the poet who was born in 1757 just two years before that other Robert – the poet Robert Burns of Ayrshire.

Frontier Life of Scotch-Irish Settlers

Although they quickly adapted to life in a new environment, the Scotch-Irish community in Londonderry, New Hampshire, maintained close links with their Scottish and Irish friends and family back home. They also kept up the way they saw and thought about the world as they had done in Europe. The Scottish and Ulster-Scottish traditions of song and speech that they were used to in the Old World were carried over to America. Like some great extended family, the community looked to the family of the original leaders the McGregors and McKeens for guidance on a number of issues. This even extended to matters of language.

Writing in 1809 Dinsmoor said, 'I am told that Capt. Hunter's wife (a McGregore) is the best Scotch dictionary in Londonderry and reads it the best.' For these people, speaking Scotch, or at least a relatively Scottish version of American English, was obviously a living and treasured phenomenon. Dinsmoor emphasised this in choosing Scotch as a medium for his poem 'Spring's Lamentation and Confession'. This tale about a high spirited, wayward dog who meets a grisly ending employs Scotch words and a Scottish verse form to vocalise the dog's fate. 'I tried to make the little rascal speak English at first, but I soon found he was far better versed in Scotch', Dinsmoor tells his readers. While this colloquial speech may indicate the dog's uncouth nature and his perceived lack of sophistication and civility as a mere animal, it also underlines that he is still viewed as part of the community. The conclusion takes on a sense of outrage at the breaking of what Dinsmoor believes is a very important thing, the harmony between people, animals and nature, when he is killed.

'There Is Something Extraordinary In That Wean'

Dinsmoor's book testifies to the deep value placed in literacy and education. Without it, the network of communication and correspondence that stretches from Scotland to the eastern expanses of the United States would never have existed. His work is a celebration of the human ability to talk, write, learn and share ideas in person and on the page. He tells us in his introduction that he was a precocious child and that his grandfather said about him, 'There is something extraordinary in that wean'. Again, 'wean' is an interesting usage to denote a child. Rather than the more familiar term 'bairn', Dinsmoor deploys what was and is an Ulster and Western Scottish form. This should alert us to the continuity of speech forms in the New World that travelled westward, just like the Dinsmoors, from Scotland, to the north of Ireland and on to America. And more importantly, there is no sense of being embarrassed about the word, it is the most fitting and homely choice available, as cherished as the memory of his grandfather's response.

Language, as one might expect is of particular interest to a poet and we should be grateful to him for recording so many words that appear to maintain their force and meaning after they crossed the Atlantic. By the time Dinsmoor published his book, Robert Burns, the Scottish poet who did so much to popularise Scottish poetry and the idea of labouring class poets in the public's imagination, was an international bestseller. Poems such as his 'To A Mouse', demonstrate how simple reflections on everyday country incidents, such as destroying a mouse's nest in a cornfield, can allow a poet to make great philosophical and comic statements about life and destiny.

> Wee, sleekit, cowrin, tim'rous beastie,
> O, what a panic's in thy breastie!
> Thou need na start awa sae hasty
>   Wi bickering brattle!
> I wad be laith to rin an' chase thee,
>   Wi' murdering pattle.

We might assume that Dinsmoor was merely copying Burns when we read similar poems in his collection. However, Dinsmoor is special, as his Scotch words and verses indicate that prior to the popularity and fashion for Scottish poetry created by Robert Burns's worldwide fame these words and verse styles were employed by American writers. For instance, when Dinsmoor was a lad of fifteen he wrote a poem about his pet dog 'Skip' in which he emphasised the sense of equality that he felt there was for all God's creatures:

> Though like a lord man o'er ye rules,
> An' bang ye round wi'chairs an' stools,
> An' bruse ye w'i the auld pot buils,
>   Mind not their powers–
> Their bodies maun gang to the mools,
>   As weel as ours.

Dinsmoor was concerned to write properly in Scotch and to observe its rules. He never treats it as slang or as poor English. Indeed, he shows his determination to further celebrate his ancestral home by adopting the genres of traditional Scottish verse for his own work. This is underscored on numerous occasions when he uses the traditional six line verse form of 'Standard

Habbie', which was later termed 'Burns Stanza' as Burns proved himself such a master in its use. This stanza form is a classic Scottish poetic vehicle, whose energy and rhythm is the poetic cousin of a jig or reel, and had been used in Scottish poetry for over two centuries prior to Dinsmoor's poem, to record touching elegies or for brilliant, devastating satire.

Scotch words and phrases matter to Dinsmoor and his correspondents as important symbols of shared culture and he was determined to make sure that his choices of specific vernacular words were understood. In addition to a glossary at the end of the collection, several of his letters which stand as headnotes to the verses, explain his choice of language. Writing to his friend, and benefactor Silas Betton, a local landowner in New Hampshire, he discusses whether, 'mools' has a singular form:

> Let not the insignificant term, 'mools' distress you – it passes very well. Mr Allen [the editor of the *Haverhill Intelligencer* in which a number of Dinsmoor's poems first appeared] told me the other day, the poem was well received in Haverhill, and much applauded amongst his readers, as far as he could learn. I think, myself, 'mools' has no singular other than ashes. But this is not discerned by the generality of our Scotch readers –They consider it to mean the same as 'moul', which is pretty generally understood earth or mould, perhaps originating from moulder, as a body mouldering in the dust.

As the letter above indicates, 'mools' has many more meanings than simply the English 'earth'. His fascination with soil can be seen to be the interest of someone from farming stock, close to and aware of the land (for example a plough has a 'moul-board' on it – a piece of equipment that he would have been very aware of). But Dinsmoor's definition seems to focus on 'mools' as the spot of land that will act as a person's final resting place. Given how much Dinsmoor is fascinated with the big questions about life and death it is a particularly apt word for him to discuss and to dignify in verse.

Robert Dinsmoor also uses Scotch as an everyday way of speaking rather than as fancy words for the showy world of poetry. So in one of his letters we see him writing, 'It will soon be, "some wee short hour ayont the twall."' (i.e beyond twelve midnight). A reader gets the feeling that he or she is getting a flavour of a whole community speaking to itself in its everyday language, as they sit out the long winter evenings in the New Hampshire forest.

Dinsmoor is keenly aware of the duties owed to family, religion and tradition in his writing. For him the poems stand as milestones of remembrance and contemplation of past times. Moreover, he loved a good fight and disputation. He believed strongly in Trinitarian Presbyterianism, i.e. that God existed in three states, as a Father creator figure, as the Holy Spirit, and that he had sent his son, Jesus to earth, who although in human form, was still part of his divine being. Other doctrines and denominations, particularly Unitarians, who did not believe Jesus to be divine, come in for strong criticism from Dinsmoor, and to those opponents he is a fiery antagonist. In that most American of celebrations, Thanksgiving Day, he makes the following statement, in a poem of the same name:

> When we of health enjoy a share,
> And feast upon some wholesome fare,
> Our hearts should rise in grateful prayer.
>   And bless the donor
> In thankful songs, let voices rare
>   Exult his honor.
>
> Perhaps in leisure hours you choose
> To pass the time, and to amuse,
> The Unitarian scheme peruse;
>   But, sir, take heed,
> Their subtle reasoning may confuse,
>   And wreck your creed.

Yet for all this, he displays a strong, simple Christian faith that is at times very tender when he writes about his children, and open and accommodating as he enjoys literary exchanges between people of many and no denomination. The theology, rather than the person was what drew out his fury. We see him as a member of a society that engages in lively philosophical discussion about religious doctrine and preaching. Things matter to him, and like our own world today there is much argument about life and death issues.

> Then in my field we would dispute 'im,
> And sometimes we would laugh and hoot 'im,
> And three miles off we could refute 'im,
>   With reasons strong,
> And with false doctrines durst impute 'im,
>   And tenets wrong.'

We can imagine Dinsmoor, almost ready to come to blows in his cornfield, taking his opponent to task in a verbal fight.

Famous Friends

The collection demonstrates Dinsmoor's popularity and wide appeal with instances of his poem published in Maine and New Hampshire newspapers. The preface was penned by his friend the famous Quaker abolitionist poet, John Greenleaf Whittier. After his death, Greenleaf described him fondly as 'a home-loving, unpretending farmer, cultivating his acres with his own horny hands, and cheering the long rainy days and winter evenings with homely rhyme'. While, this may be a romanticised portrait, the evident esteem of Whittier for his friend and possible mentor shines through. Whittier may well have wished to downgrade Dinsmoor's influence upon him, as it appears one of Whittier's first poems was published in Dinsmoor's collection, something which Whittier does not dwell too much upon in later reminiscences. The numerous correspondents listed within the poems highlight how extensive Dinsmoor's reputation was extended throughout the north-east of the United States.

Dinsmoor spoke to and for many people. His book shows all his various voices and moods. His sense of fun and the ridiculous shines through, as does his enthusiasm for life and his strong sincerity in all the things he believes in. To some he is a concerned parent, relative or friend catching up with a loved one, offering advice and practical support. To others he is a backwoods politician making his point simply and sternly. And to all he stands as a representative of his State and country, aware that his work has the potential to reach out to the world. His poem, 'The Author To his Friend, Col. Silas Dinsmoor, of Mobile, Alabama, In Scotch, The Dialect of Their Ancestors' encapsulates his sense of where he has come from and where he is going,

>Our great grandsire fam'd and rever'd
>In Londonderry lies interr'd!
>There, at his head wi' kind regard,
>>We'd pile some stanes,
>Renew the turf, and right the swaird,
>>That co'ers his banes!
>
>Whan we our ancient line retrace,
>He was the first o' a' our race,
>Cauld Erin ca'his native place,
>>O' name Dinsmore!
>And first that saw wi' joyfu' face,
>>Columbia's shore!*
>
>Though death our ancestors has cleeket,
>An under clods them closely steeket;
>Their native tongue we yet wad speak it,
>>Wi accent glib;
>And mark the place their chimney's reeket,
>>Like brithers sib.

For all his determination to record his family history honestly and with dignity, he was not afraid to make fun of his cherished traditions either. One of the most famous events in seventeenth-century Irish history is probably The Siege of Derry when the Protestant Apprentice boys of the city, who supported King William, shut the gates against the Earl of Antrim's Jacobite troops. Everyone in Londonderry, New Hampshire in the early eighteenth century had either been at the siege or was the son or grandson/daughter of one of those inside Derry in the winter of 1688/9. Rev. McGregor, the town's Presbyterian pastor, as a twelve

---

* Columbia: A poetic name for America.

year old boy had rung the bell in St Columb's Cathedral when the merchant ship, The Mountjoy, broke the boom that was placed across the River Foyle. One might think that Dinsmoor would have sentimentalised this event, but this is far from the case, evidence perhaps of his dual heritage not always necessarily being in harmony with itself. His poem 'Antiquity – The Auld Gun' describes the history of a rifle which has been handed down from the siege times and then used in America in the Indian Wars and the War of Independence. In Dinsmoor's poem it speaks as recognisably as an American object, proud yet coarsely aware of its Yankee sentiments, despite all of its Scotch-Irish heritage:

> Whan master brought me to this land,
> I aye stood charged at his right hand;
> Nae Indian warrior e'er could stand,
>   Against Dinsmore!
> My hail was death, at his command,
>   Wi' thundering roar!
>
> Me as his ain, I aye could claim
> At "number four," he rais'd my fame,
> Wi's Jocteleg – when far frae hame,
>   He rudely cut
> Th' initials o' his honor'd name
>   Upon my butt!

This reference either to the house number, presumably of the Dinsmoor farmstead, or to his military squad's number, takes us away from the great events of earth shattering wars to the domestic world of the farmer and hunter, carving his name proudly and roughly into his gun stock with his hunting knife (jocteleg).

Although Dinsmoor wrote partly in Scotch and had a proud awareness of his ancestry it would be unfair to claim that he was merely imitative or sentimental about either Scotland or Ulster. Indeed, Ireland is viewed as a cold place theologically, socially and geographically and he considered himself very fortunate to have been born a Yankee. His discussion of Europe suggests much satisfaction to have been an inhabitant of the New World. Although much inspiration is sought from Scotland – as ancestral home and literary fatherland – his attempts to write as an American with a recognisably American accent are soon apparent. Even the debt to Robert Burns is questioned by Dinsmoor in the preface:

> [while Burns's] work inspired him he did not pretend to be anywhere else than he found himself – his work has an honesty about it ... Burns is the bonny Doon flowing through the banks and braes of Scotland, and Dinsmoor is the Merrimack passing through our western soil and reflecting from its crystal bed the western scenery through which it passes.

His focus is always on things American. In political terms, he was a supporter of the Federalist cause, a movement that sought to support the American Constitution against external and internal threats. While some of his newspaper verse might be said to be linked to the transitory nature of small town events, his determination to articulate his deeply held point of view is always apparent. Dinsmoor was not merely a literary campaigner, but someone who had worked tirelessly to create and maintain his vision of America. A veteran of the American Revolution – at eighteen he enlisted as 'a fifer in Captain Reynolds' company' and he adds in his introduction, 'At twenty I was at the taking of Burgoyne'. In the lines that he addressed to 'Lt. David Gregg on the Return of the soldiers from Bennington' he portrays his locale as an entirely committed patriot centre, 'On every side I hear a cheerful sound,/Gladness and mirth this morning doth abound.'

Dinsmoor was never in doubt about where his allegiance might lie and in his writing expressed the enthusiasm that he and others felt for the American cause:

> When British laws would us enthrall,
> Our country for defence did call;
> Then martial fire inspir'd us all,
>   To arms we flew;
> And as a soldier, stand or fall,
>   I went with you.

His work celebrates the singularity, freedom and plenty of America; and his poems that commemorate these ideals anticipate the other great American poets of the nineteenth century: Emerson, Longfellow, Whittier, Whitman and Dickinson. New Hampshire, to Dinsmoor is a sort of Promised Land to which the Scotch-Irish people had been delivered.

> New Hampshire's sons, with plenty blest,
> May by their social fireside stay,
> By no fell tyrant's hand opprest,
> 'Till winter's storms have howled away.'
> And not just The Promised Land but also The Land of
>   Milk and Honey.
> 'Then smiling wives wi'a' their brood,
> Shall grace our board in jovial mood,
> An' wi'us sup the luscious food,
>   Like Yankees true,
> Syne we will praise the name o'Gude,
>   When we are fu'.

However, there is another element to Dinsmoor's poetry that places him beyond an unthinking sort of patriotism. In his determination to be a rustic bard, he invests his poetry in the authentic, vernacular culture of New Hampshire life in all its diverse complexity. His work speaks of simple noble family values but it also captures a sense of the possibilities of America as a subject for Art and Poetry. Beneath all the trappings of Scotch verse and language, we see a vibrant American identity emerging.

FRANK FERGUSON
ALISTER McREYNOLDS

INCIDENTAL POEMS
ACCOMPANIED WITH LETTERS AND A FEW SELECT
PIECES, MOSTLY ORIGINAL FOR THEIR ILLUSTRATION
TOGETHER WITH A PREFACE AND SKETCH OF THE
AUTHOR'S LIFE.

By Robert Dinsmoor, the 'Rustic Bard'.
Haverhill, A.W. Thayer Printer, 1828.

District of New Hampshire – to wit:

District Clerk's Office

BE IT REMEMBERED. That on the twenty-third day of January A.D. 1828, in the fifty-second year of the independence of the United States of America, Robert Dinsmoor of the said District, has deposited in the Office the Title of a Book the Right whereof he claims as author, in the words following, to wit:

Incidental Poems
accompanied with letters and a few select pieces, mostly original for their illustration together with a preface and sketch of the author's life.

In conformity to the Act of Congress of the United States, entitled 'An Act for the Encouragement of Learning, by securing the Copies of Maps, Charts and Books, to the Authors and Proprietors of such Copies during the times therein mentioned:' and also to an Act entitled 'An Act supplementary to an Act. entitled, An Act for the Encouragement of Learning, by securing the Copies of Maps, Charts and Books to the Authors and Proprietors of such Copies during the times therein mentioned, and extending the Benefits thereof to the Arts of Designing, Engraving and Etching Historical and other Prints.'

CHARLES W. CUTTER,
Clerk of the District Court of the United States,
for the District of New-Hampshire.

Original Preface

THE work which is now presented to the public, is strictly what its title page imports – a volume of incidental poems. Most of them were suggested by events which took place in the author's family or among his more intimate acquaintance and friends. They might be well characterized by calling them extracts in poetry from a sentimental journal. In preparing them for the press, less has been done by "way of improvement," than would perhaps have been expected. In this, however, we have acted from a principle long since adopted, and strengthened by the experience of every year, that ordinarily, no one can so well express another's sentiments, feelings or judgment, as himself. There is with most men, if we may be allowed the expression, an idiosyncrasy of thought and style. It is this, which by exhibiting the "lights and shades" in which moral truths are contemplated by different men, more than any new truths, that gives us such an interest in the almost countless numbers of authors who have favored the world with writings on almost every subject connected with the opinions and responsibilities of men. Yet the moment one begins to change the words, alter the arrangement, strike out or introduce sentences, something of this peculiarity is sacrificed; and with it something of the interest the work was calculated to excite, and something of the instruction it was calculated to convey. With these views we have been careful not to present to the public the Bard's ideas clothed in our language, but throughout where some consideration paramount to the sentiment already expressed, did not require, have permitted him to express his own ideas in his own, though sometimes in a rustic way.

That the reader may the better understand some expressions in the following poems, we judge it proper to observe, that Silas Betton, Esq., late of Salem, N. H., without having previously informed the author, did copy out a manuscript volume of the poems and letters of the Bard, with the intention of publishing them. And after he had mostly prepared the work for the press, presented it to him for his inspection and revision. The feelings which were produced in the author's mind upon receiving this volume, as described by himself, cannot but prove interesting to all. Nor will any one read some of the closing pieces of this volume, written since the printing commenced, without a sensible desire that it may escape those severe strictures which are sometimes made upon the writings of others, not reflecting how deeply they wound the feelings without affording any light or instruction which can help the author to mend.

It is but just to observe, that the Bard was under great obligation to his very particular friend, mentioned above, for the encouragement and help he received from him, and it is gratifying to observe how sensible he has always been of this obligation; nor ought the fact to be passed over, that the people in Haverhill, when several of his pieces had been published in their village paper, raised a handsome subscription for his benefit, as a testimony of their sense of his worth, and just acknowledgement of the obligation they were under for the entertainment he had afforded them.

The reader is here presented with the effusions of a mind which has taken its poetical impressions fresh from nature. The word nature, in the vocabulary of criticism, is frequently used for the most polished productions of art, that perfection of art by which art is concealed, and nature imitated. In the present instance, it is literally true, that the author of these poems wrote from the untutored impulses of his own mind. His right to poetry, was derived from the God that made him. He describes the landscapes he has seen, and the transactions he has been engaged in, and if his muse in some degree has a more homely and rustic air, than that of more learned poets, it is because he is profoundly original. He incorporates with every verse the peculiarities of his own mind.

The art of poetry has been described as the art of copying from nature. It is ranked by Aristotle, among the arts of imitation. But many of the objects of nature are not worthy of copying; they are too plain, too vulgar, too unawakening to interest in any transcription, and hence the poet is obliged not only to copy, but to select. The business then of an original writer is the compound employment of making his descriptions and pictures resemble the patterns, and judging what patterns are worthy of imitation. We shall find there is a middle point where these two principles meet; and in giving each their proper portion, consists the great art of writing well. If you copy promiscuously, your book will indeed be nature, but nature in her naked deformity; nature stripped of all interest; nature, from which every eye turns away, if you carry your selections too far, if you are fastidious in carrying your points of similitude, you may make a beautiful description, but it will be almost ideal; the reader will not trace the resemblance, because there will be fewer objects to compare. To aim at this middle, is the object of every good writer, and he departs from it on one side or the other, according as he has cultivated his genius or his judgment. Shakespeare, in the character of the Nurse, in Romeo and Juliet, has imitated nature; but the imitation is too close; the language is too homely; it is too much like the chattering of a real nurse, and every judicious reader, wishes the picture had been less exact, or never attempted. Mr. Addison, in the character of Cato, has intended to imitate nature; but, in has care to select only the sublimest parts of nature, he has made Cato scarcely a man. He is almost an allegorical being, an abstract of philosophy, uttering the sentiments of stoical grandeur and pride. Addison and Shakespeare equally aim at copying nature; and they are both governed by a principle of selection, (for even Shakespeare did not write all that a foolish nurse would say,) but they differ in the proportion with which they compound these principles. Shakespeare had too little selection. Addison too much. To compound them correctly, is the sublimest achievement of intellectual man.

If the illustrious minds of Shakespeare and Addison failed of hitting this delicate centre of perfection, it is not to be wondered at, if a rustic bard, should not always satisfy the critic in executing the difficult task. It must be confessed, he verges to the same side with Shakespeare. He imitates nature with too little selection. He certainly has one of the qualities of the greatest poets; and though we are aware that this quality may be pushed to such an extreme as to lose much of its value, yet we cannot but hope that these poems, will have some power to arrest the bosom, alive to the impulses of simplicity and truth.

Our author found his way to poetry by the suggestions of his own mind. He felt the inspiration, and he obeyed it. He is strictly an original; and like every other original writer, he shews less skill in selecting the beautiful parts of nature for imitation, than felicity in conveying to the reader the impressions which he feels. He is the poet of domestic life as it is exhibited in New England. He makes us see and feel the incidents of a farmer's house, together with the influence of sorrow or joy which they had over the heart. The picture comes to us neither improved by time, nore mellowed by distance, but we know it to be just. There is no art, no refinement, no sublimity in his lines, but there is a fresh importation of images from the living world. He opens to us his fireside, and shews the changes of his family; he reveals the secrets of his heart, and gives us an interest in his hopes and disappointments, his perplexities and his reliefs. Even his religious opinions, and his censures on those who deny his favorite doctrines, though sometimes verging to harshness, are yet interesting as the faithful portrait of a New England puritan. His muse, it must be allowed, is occasionally too coarse; she verges too often to naked nature, and repulsive rusticity. But she is also honest, plain and pathetic; often striking, and always pure and pious. She is a nymph, dressed not in the classic wreaths of Greece and Rome; nor does she wear the roses and lilies of Italy or England. Her garland is white-weed, a less fanciful plant, but the production of our own soil. We hear not the nightingales of a foreign grove, but the Bob'o'lincoms of our own.

In claiming for our author so much originality, perhaps the reader may be inclined to dispute that point with us. It may be said that he writes in the Scotch dialect, and with a manifest reference to Burns. Respecting his using the Scotch dialect, we would remark, that he is really of Scotch descent, though of American birth; and began to write poetry before he knew that Burns existed. Every one acquainted with New England customs, knows, that in a farmer's house, you commonly see, a Bible and Watt's Psalm-Book, his Lyric Poems, Pope's Essay on Man, Pilgrim's Progress, and an Almanac. This constitutes their library; and from sources like these, our author probably derived all his juvenile literature. After he had been in the habit of writing poetry for some time, a friend sent him a copy of the poems of Burns. They were congenial spirits; and it is easy to see that the present fired his mind. It is impossible for us to be conversant with a favorite book without feeling our minds, in some degree, modified by it. But instead of charging him with imitating Burns, we are rather astonished at the good sense and discrimination, which led him to make proper use of his favorite author. Whatever similitude there may be between them, he shews peculiar judgment in not transfusing a single sample of foreign scenery into his native land. If he resembles Burns, it is with all the diversity of the two countries in which each were born. Burns is the bonny Doon flowing through the banks and braes of Scotland, and Dinsmoor is the Merrimack passing through our western soil and reflecting from its crystal bed the western scenery through which it passes.

Before surrendering our author to the public, we must protest against making his naked simplicity, his pure nature, an object of censure or ridicule. We acknowledge this would be easy; but the facility of the work should make it contemptible. A correct author hazards nothing; with no novelty of manner he cannot be ridiculous. Our poet hazards every thing; and though he has not always preserved the decorum of poetry, it may be found by the candid critic, that he has secured some happier beauties by not submitting to its restraints.

Life Of The Author Written By Himself, In A Letter To Silas Betton, Esq. Of Salem, N.H.

WINDHAM, January, 1817

DEAR SIR:— THE volume you sent me by the hand of our friend Park, in manuscript, was duly received. The superscription on the wrapper, I instantly discerned to be your own hand writing; but for what intent you had sent me such a large book, I could not guess. I soon broke the seal, and with a trembling hand, turned over the blank leaves at beginning, which I afterwards found were left as room for an introduction. The first line of writing which met my eye, was, "The following is the first effusion of the Rustic Bard," which appeared in print. — While I read that, I actually felt my heart beat. As I continued to turn the leaves, for I did not stop to read the whole, I frequently met with "The Editor," "The Author," "The Compiler," "The Poet," &c. By that time, I am sure I grew pale, and as I still kept turning the leaves, I found notes and remarks, in all the form of a printed volume, except the impression of the type. What, thought I, can this mean? Has the Squire prepared for the press? Still I continued to turn along, and there I found the satires in "Skinflint," with all their invectives, "Spring's Lamentation and Confession," and another piece, which I will not name. At that, my knees smote together like Belshazzar's! I then closed the book, and laid it on my desk. In a few days, I was able to take it out, and read your last letter to me, having recovered a little from the shock. Although in part of it, there may appear in the eyes of the world, or in the eyes of some, a degree of levity, inconsistent with the character of an author of serious sentiment, yet I think upon it a fair and candid examination, it will be found that the author in no instance has reproached religion, nor cast a dart at true morality. The contrary only is lacerated. Several pieces were written on trivial occasions, with no other view than to amuse myself, and cultivate a genius for poetry; and I hope, some allowance will be made on that account.

You propose to write an introduction, and by what you have said, I expect you mean to be my biographer. You threaten to expose some of my foibles, and point particularly at my orthodoxy. This matter, sir, I hope you will handle with the greatest tenderness and delicacy. My orthodoxy has been handed down to me by my progenitors, as the Urim and Thummin, held sacred by the family since the reformation from popery in Scotland.

Not many years since, a short time after my uncle John Dinsmoor's death, his son John received a letter from his friend Robert Dinsmore, of Bellywattick, Ireland, which gave a proper, and I believe an authentic history of the Dinsmoor family, ever since their emigration from Scotland to Ireland. That letter was in 'Squire Dinsmoor's possession when he went to live in Londonderry. I make no doubt I could find it among his papers if I knew where to look for it. It contained the Dinsmoors' beautiful coat of arms.

My father's great grandfather was an emigrant from a place in Scotland, called Achenmead, near the river Tweed, and was the only one of the name who ever settled in Ireland from that country. He took his residence in or near Bellywattick, I think in the county of Antrim, and I have been informed lately by a nephew of Colonel Means, who left that country not long since, that a number of Dinsmoors live there to this day. From that man, I think his name was John, sprang all the Dinsmoors ever known in Ireland or America, which are now almost innumerable. My father's grandfather, John Dinsmoor, was the oldest son of this Scotchman, and came to this country about the time the first settlers of Londonderry came. He is yet remembered by many of the old people, and very respectfully called Daddy Dinsmoor. But, whether from accident, I know not, he was landed at a place called Georges, where was an English fort, in the district of Maine. There he built a house, and the Indians which traversed these woods, (I believe they were of the Penobscot tribe,) became very familiar with him, calling him and themselves all one brother. This was about the commencement of a war between Great Britain and France.

One day, when Daddy Dinsmoor was shingling his house, the Indians surrounded it with the war-whoop, ordering him down, saying, "no longer one brother, you go Canada." He was taken and kept with them three months. The Chief's name was John, and Daddy Dinsmoor became his waiter, and "found grace in his sight." On a certain day, Captain John was called to attend a council of war, and in his absence, old Daddy was accused by two squaws, of being seen on a certain point of land near the shore, in conference with some Englishmen, and although in the absence of the chief, he was condemned to be burnt. He was accordingly bound to the tree, and the fatal pile made around him, and that instant to be set on fire, when providentially, the captain returned, and commanded his execution should be delayed until inquiry should be made with respect to the truth of the charge, alleging if it were true, their tracks could be seen, as the place was a very sandy point.

The charge was soon proved to be false, and he was reprieved. The last three days he was with them, they traveled almost night and day, a great part of the time at a "dog trot," carrying their canoes with them. When they had a river to cross, as soon as the captain was seated in the Bark, it was Daddy Dinsmoor's office to push it off and jump in after; and having performed this duty at a certain river, the captain being resolved to set him at liberty, forbade him step in. He plead for leave to get in but the chief replied "No, you much honest man, John — you walk Boston." Daddy answered, "The Indians will kill me." The captain then told him how, and where he could find a cave in a rock, where he must lie three days, and in that time the Indians would all be past. He gave him some bear's grease and a few nuts, saying "Indians and French have all this land, you walk Boston, John, then take English canoe, walk under your own country – you much honest man, John."

My father's grandfather, then took his solitary way, and found the rock as the captain had told him. When he lay there three days and nights, he saw the Indians pass tribe after tribe, until they were all passed. Then he arose from his cave, and thought he must die of hunger; but by chance, or by providence, rather, he found some cranberries, which supported him until he arrived at fort

George. From thence, he got a passage to Boston, and from thence he visited his old friends and countrymen in Nutfield, now Londonderry. They had all been acquainted with Daddy Dinsmoor, in Ireland. For the respect they had for the man, and perhaps moved by the narrative of his sufferings, which no one doubted, the proprietors of Londonderry, made a gift of one hundred acres of excellent land, and confirmed it by deed, to him and his heirs forever.

He was a mason by trade, and built there for himself a stone house. Then he sent to Ireland for his wife and children, which I believe were all he ever had, and they by a former wife. Their names were Robert and Elizabeth. Robert had by then his wife, Margaret Orr, four children, named John, Mary, Elizabeth, and Robert. Elizabeth had two by her husband, John Hopkins, named James and Margaret. They all arrived safe in 1730. Old Daddy divided his farm equally between his two children. He and his wife lived in the stone house with their son Hopkins. There Elizabeth bare John, Robert, Nancy and Ruth, wife of the aged minstrel, lately deceased.

In May 1731, my father, William Dinsmoor, was born, and two years after, Samuel, whom my father always esteemed as the flower of the flock. Daddy Dinsmoor lived ten years after my father was born. He and his son being both masons, they built a number of stone houses in the town, which served as garrisons in the Indian war. (And I really believe, that his once being an Indian captive, was his inducement to build a stone house on his own land, in Londonderry.) The remains of many of those houses are to be seen at this day; and a great many stone chimneys, as no brick could then be had. His name was ever held in honor by all who knew him.

Soon after Daddy Dinsmoor's death, my grandfather, Robert Dinsmoor, with his family, removed to the place where your sister Ruth now lives; and there the family prospered wonderfully for about ten years. He was lieutenant of the first company of militia formed in Windham, under Captain James Gilmore; and my grandfather Cochran, was ensign. At the decease of the two senior officers, ensign Cochran became the captain, and commanded the company in Windham since my remembrance.

My grandfather Dinsmoor, had accumulated a good property, and intended settling his four sons on and about Jenny's Hill, close by him; but died very unexpectedly of the fever and ague, I think in the 59th year of his age, and about ten years after he moved to Jenny's Hill.

In about two years after his death, Samuel died of a consumption, in the 20th year of his age. My father mourned for him all the days of his life. In a letter which he wrote to his sister, Mary Nesmith, was this paragraph, which my memory still retains. His writings in general are lost by the carelessness of his friends, and the rats and mice in his own closet.

> When I reflect on days of yore,
>   When Samie my dear brither,
> Amang my feet did pile a store,
>   O' learning up thegether;
> Whan, ah! poor me! might had my share,
>   Had I na been o'er stout;
> It seem'd sae far beneath my care,
>   I for it wadna lout.
> Had I improved that precious time,
>   As he did aft invite,
> I wadna need to shame this rhyme,
>   Wi' ugly scrabbled write.
> Whist, muse! be silent, haud your tongue –
>   Past time will ne'er come back –
> The time that's present, or to come,
>   Let us the best o't mak'.

My father, William Dinsmoor, at the age of 24, married John Cochran's oldest child, Elizabeth, in her twentieth year, by whom he had six sons and four daughters. Their names were Janet, Robert, Margaret, John, Samuel, Mary, William, Issac, and Elizabeth. Between Margaret and John, died a child in infancy, which was the only child he ever buried. No very remarkable occurrence happened in my father's family during his life. He began the world with little more than his land. He was a wonderful mechanical genius, and made all the wooden utensils both for his house and farm. The difficulties that attended the revolutionary war, bore hard upon him; he was then in debt for the land I now live on, but was fortunate enough to be able to pay all his debts, was possessor of a good estate, lived comfortably, saw his children all married agreeably to his mind, and settled in decent circumstances. He often served the town as selectmen, &c., and was many years a military officer. His highest commission, which is now in good liking, was a lieutenant-colonel of the alarm list. He died in November, 1801, in the 71st year of his age.

You wish to know "the eventful era when I was born." I was born October 7, 1757. If there are any other circumstances relative to me, and my own particular family, which you are ignorant of, I doubt they will be hardly worth your notice. I never like to hear a man tell great things about himself. Were I to tell you I was always thought to have a tenacious memory from infancy, it would look like boasting. If I were to tell you that my friends discerned marks in me of a philosopher, at a very early age, this would look like ostentation. Although I know I made some remarks when but a child, to my grandmother, as she led me by the hand to my grandfather's one clear moon-light evening, respecting the sun, moon, and stars. She related our conversation to the old gentleman, and my ideas nearly astonished them both; and I remember of hearing my grandfather say, "There is something extraordinary in that wean." I will tell you however, an anecdote of myself, which I heard my uncle Cochran mention but a few months since. I know the fact. I was often at my grandfather's when a child, being their first grandson. One day I went off, without telling any person where, or for what, to explore the little brook that ran between my uncle Robin's and my grandfather's. I was not at that time five years old. I went up the stream to find where it came from; and at length I found it sprang out of the ground at the bottom of the hill, near where the old schoolhouse since stood. You know the place. Then I went downstream to find where it went to. I followed it through my grandfather's fields, through Uncle Dinsmoor's swamp, into the great swamp, where it fell into Sterret's meadow brook; thence I followed it through all the meadows and crossed the road at Mr. William Jameson's, into his great swamp, and there it joined another great stream, which was Mr. Tuft's mill brook. There I despaired of finding the end of it. I then returned back to my grandfather's, and found them all hunting, and crying after me, thinking I was lost, for I had been gone a great while. I came hopping up to my grandmother, not feeling the least trouble. When she saw me, she cried, "Where have you been you rogue?" I answered, I was trying to find where the little brook went to.

Unfortunately, for me, I had no opportunity of being a day at school till after I was nine years old. My parents, however, had been careful to learn me many little lessons. At that time, the Rev. Simon Williams was ordained pastor of the town, and for the improvement of singing, Mr. James Aiken was hired to teach a singing school every evening, for a month. And a few of the neighbors hired him to teach their children to read by day for the same length of time. I went to school every day, and my father carried me to the singing-school every evening. Through the help of my father, a lover of music, but no singer, I learned to find my *mi*, and call the notes in any tune. I believe I could sing every tune in the little Bailey book, and several in William's collection. Soon after this, Master Sauce, an old British soldier, being discharged at the end of the old French war, was hired to teach a school in our neighborhood for four years. At the age of eleven years, I could repeat the shorter and longer catechism verbatim. Those with the scripture proofs annexed to them confirmed me in the orthodoxy of my forefathers, and I hope I shall ever remain a lasting evidence of the truth of what the wise man has said – " Train up a child in the way he should go, and when he is old he will not depart from it."

Some years after master Sauce left us, master M'Keen was employed to teach in the same schoolhouse. He was a man of profound erudition; but very dilatory in attending. If he took in hand to catch a squirrel by the way, he would do it if it took him half the forenoon. My father sent me to school always when he could spare me until the revolutionary war came on. I could then read, write and cypher tolerably. I could also sing and make poetry, and might have been a good mathematician, but for the love I had to M*** P****, and the muses. In those days, I wrote "Skip's Last Advice," and some other puerile poems.

After master M'Keen left Windham, my father made me a kind of pedagogue in his family during the winter season. When I was eighteen, I spent three months in the army, as fifer in captain Reynold's company. At twenty, I was at the taking of Burgoyne. From that time, I was employed as a school-master five winters in the neighborhood. At twenty-five I was married to my beloved Polly Park, aged twenty-one. She lived with me sixteen years and five months to a day. She left with me eleven children. The youngest seven weeks old; besides we had two buried infants. In twelve years after the death of the dear woman, I lost Betty. On the last day of the year 1801, I was married to Mary Anderson, a woman noted for her economy and good character, with whom I have lived comfortably. I was an elder in the church before I was thirty years old. By this time I am sure you will be heartily sick of my trifling detail. If you can find any thing in it worthy of a place in my biography, you are welcome to make use of it.

A Letter From Robert Dinsmore,* Of Bellywattick, Ireland, To John Dinsmore Of Londonderry, Containing An Account Of The Dinsmore Family, Dated Bellywattick, August 12, 1794

MY DEAR SIR: In July last, I received your affectionate letter of 22nd February, 1794, where you have given me a full and clear answer to my letter of May 12th, 1793, which was directed to your honoured father. But, alas! no more! May I not bid adieu to North America. Submission is a duty, therefore, I shall only add – I shall go to him, but he shall not return to me. It gives me consolation that he has left a son and heir, blest with his principles and talents. I see you feel for the commotions of Europe, and for the arbitrary proceedings of our government in particular. You give them hard names. Indeed, so could we, but dare not; we are brought to submission indeed. While our lives are protected by the laws, we must submit our property to the discretion of government without a murmur or complaint. Provided our taxes, which are heavy, were disposed of for internal defence of our country, and encouragement of our trade and manufactures, we would pay more cheerfully. But when we see it levied to support a ruinous war, that we think Great Britain had nothing to do with, we complain the more. At this moment, the eyes of all Ireland are looking earnestly for the completion of your peace with Great Britain, on which the trade of Ireland much depends. We know that you have sent a late commissioner from congress to the court of Great Britain, a Mr. Jay; but as nothing has yet transpired in respect to Ireland, I must be silent.

  I had a long letter from your brother Silas, in May last, which I answered. It raises my pride to find that there is a Dinsmore in any part of the globe, so capable of composition, as I see the writer of this letter to be. The more so, when I can truly call him friend and cousin.

---

* Dinsmore and Dinsmoor, are different ways of writing the names, adopted by different branches of the family. The former is consided the true spelling.

As to your request concerning the genealogy of our family, you have been pretty fortunate indeed in calling on me, as I assure you there is not a man living within the reach of my knowledge, that can go as far up in that description as I can. Nevertheless, it may be short of what history could afford. Please take the following. My grandfather was born on the mean land of Scotland, near the river Tweed; the son of a wealthy farmer, as I suppose from his style, being called the Laird of Achenmead, as he had tenants under him. He had two sons, of which my grandfather was the second, whose name was John. He left his father's house in the 17th year of his age. I suppose he must have eloped, as he brought no property with him, as I often heard, save a grey bonnet, of great extent, with striped woollen hose, and a small cane in his hand. This is your original in Ireland, and mine; and all by the name of Dinsmore here, or elsewhere, that belong to that stock. Therefore, you will be ready to say, we have little to boast of. But stay a little, my dear friend, and let us go a little higher and return to Scotland. You see, as above, we are sprung from a farmer. Will this give us any dignity? Yes – the most ancient, the most honorable in civil life. The second man in creation was a farmer. Cain was a tiller of the ground. What are monarchs? What are Kings, Dukes, Lords and Earls? What was Alexander, or Philip of Macedonia, but murdering vagabonds! The character of a farmer is far above this all. Stop but the farmer and his culture, and you will sweep off the human race at one stroke. So you see that the farmer's station is exalted above all others. Therefore our pedigree is higher than any other whatever.

I must crave your patience. Suffer me then to return to my grandfather and his offspring, of which you are a sprout. This man had four sons, John, Adam, Robert and Samuel. John was the first that migrated to America of the name, and the first that struck a stick in Londonderry. This man was your grandfather's father, and my uncle, who surmounted many difficulties in providing a large and free estate for his offspring, and in the attempt, was made an Indian captive.

Permit me to observe a circumstance with respect to my grandfather's leaving his father's house without any property, which may elucidate the hint before observed, respecting it, which is this – I never heard this man give any other reason or cause for his leaving his father's house, but this; that his father obliged him, and that uncovered, he hold the off stirrup of his elder brother's saddle, when he mounted his horse. A subordination that appeared not to agree with this man's proud heart. May it not be an heirship entailed on his offspring? And if so, whether virtue or vice, I leave with you to determine, although I am no advocate for virtue or vice being hereditary. To conclude then, this man lived until he was 99 years of age. He was fifty years married, and twenty-nine years a widower, which ended his life, much respected by all who was acquainted with him, for his piety, morals and good sense. Now, sir, I have gone as far as memory could assist me in answering your request. But there is yet something remains which may gratify your inquisitive mind, in the line of heraldry. The Dinsmore coat of arms, is a farm, laid down on a plate, of a green colour, with three wheat sheaves set upright in the centre of a yellow color, all emblematical of husbandry and agriculture.

ROBERT DINSMORE

The Poems of Robert Dinsmoor

EDITED BY
Frank Ferguson

Skip's Last Advice

Written in the seventeenth year of the author's age, on his father's favourite old dog, who had survived his 15th year. It was sent with the following note, to William Dinsmoor, the bard's uncle, who had requested a copy of it.

> At your request, kind sir, I send it,
> Skip's last advice – I long since penn'd it,
>   In honor to his name.
> He was a dog of noble spirit,
> Possessing talents, worth and merit,
>   And died in honest fame.
> The rational creation may
>   Learn wisdom from the brute –
> Profound instruction they convey,
>   Sometimes in language mute.
> Take heed thou, and read thou
>   This moral from my page,
> And see now, with me now,
>   A base degenerate age.

Introduction

> THIS poor auld dog liv'd mony a year,
> But now he did begin to fear
> That death about the doors was creepin',
> To whip him off when he was sleepin';
> For now he was baith deaf an' dumb,
> An' cou'dna hear when death wad come.
> When he was young, baith spry an' nimble,
> The fear o' beasts ne'er made him tremble;
> He try'd to keep the corn frae bears,
> An' help'd us ay to sing our prayers;
> But now his teeth were a' worn out,
> An' him grown weak instead of stout,
> He cou'dna sing he was sae weak,
> An' I took pity for his sake.
> He turn'd his een to me inviting,
> An' sign'd to me to do his writing;

I took the hint, an' gat my pen,
But what to write I knew not then.
I by acqaintance knew him well,
An' by his looks his thoughts could tell,
What he advis'd, I to befriend'm,
In Scottish rhyme have rightly pend'em –
From those who want to hear these lines,
I crave th' attention o' their minds: –

Tent weel! for 'tis SKIP's last advice!
He warns ye a' now to be wise;
Take heed, for he'll no tell you't twice,
  For now he's gawin'
To lea' the filthy fleas an' lice,
  That us'd to gnaw'im.

After breakfast he lay down;
Quoth he, "I fear I shall die soon,
Because I canna sing my tune,
  I us'd to sing,
To a' the hills and vallies round
  Like bells wad ring.

Hear me a' sizes o' my kind,
Baith young an' auld, keep this in mind,
An' hearken to what I've designed
  Now to advise ye:
Be guid, an' they'll be hard to find,
  That will despise ye.

Do a' you're able for your bluid,
And forward a' your master' guid –
You ought to do't since you're allow'd
  To serve mankind;
The best that e'er on four feet stood,
  This law shall find.

Let generations yet to breed,
Keep minds o' this, when we are dead!

I'm guan the gate alack wi' speed,
    O' a' the earth!
Wow! but they're simpletons indeed
    Wha live in mirth.

Don't you like those your guid time spend,
But ay think on your latter end;
If you've done ill, try to amend,
    An' gi'e ay praise,
An' thank the Ane wha did you send
    Sae mony days.

Though like a lord man o'er ye rules,
An' bang ye round wi' chairs an' stools,
An' bruise ye wi' the auld pot buils,
    Mind not their powers –
Their bodies maun gang to the mools,
    As weel as ours.

Now ere I quat, I'll ask ye a'
If deacons this a fau't can ca'
An' for the same hoist me awa'
    Unto the Session,
An' gar me satisfy their law
    For my transgression?

Gif ye say na, then I'll believ't,
An' never let mysel' be griev't,
Nor o' my rest at night be reav't,
    Nor be concern'd;
But say it is a lesson priev't,
    Ay to be learn'd.

I maun hae done, farewell, adieu!
Farewell to master Billy too,
I hae na breath to name enou;
    Death's come to plunder –
He's taken me for ane I trow,
    Sae I knock under."

An Answer To Dr John Park's Letter, Accompanying A Present Of Burns's "Reliques"

My favourite friend and cousin kind,
Your soul seems still with mine entwin'd
A constant friend in you I find,
    Without defection;
Your verse brings scenes that're past to mind –
    Sweet recollection!

I thank you, sir, for every favor,
Of which you've made me the receiver,
Since you of "Burns" so kind and clever,
    Make me the owner,
My grateful heart besure shall never
    Forget the donor.

Hail, memory! friend to friendship true,
Half of our joys we owe to you!
Past pleasing scenes then bring to view,
    By 'cute reflection;
So lovers may their pangs renew,
    By retrospection.

Yes, Jonny, I remember well,
I taught you, little words to spell,
And sat as master, (strange to tell!)
    In place of better,
And learn'd you how to hold a quill,
    And form a letter.

To the old schoolhouse you would come
Through drifts of snow, with fingers numb
Though uncle Joe would help you some,
    But growing colder,
The gladly I would take you home,
    Upon my shoulder.

And if by chance I'd stump and fall,
Then you were buried, hat and all,
Nor did I mind the pain at all,
    Though each a hand freeze,
If I could meet my darling Poll
    At uncle Andrew's.

Perhaps to please you, I'd rehearse
Skip's last advice in limping verse,
The emulation did you pierce
    With rapture new –
Your virgin muse then riving fierce,
    Sang "Robert's Shoe".

Your docile powers fast growing strong,
Though scarce discerning right from wrong,
To Williams's you trudg'd along.
    On woody road.
And Latin scholars rank'd among –
    Your book, a load.

Then S**** first began to preach,
And after fame did wring and reach,
And old Arminius' tenets teach,
    By his false rule;
And Calvin's system tear and stretch,
    And ridicule.

For fear your mind would take th' infection,
I set myself for your protection –
On Calvinistic predilection,
    My mind was bent;
And quoted texts for your direction,
    With long comment.

Good old Preceptor would declaim,
"Rigid and moderate" was his theme,
We all must quake at Hopkins' name,
    Pernicious man!

And Edwards, of immortal fame,
     Was of his clan.

Then in my field we would dispute'im,
And sometimes we would laugh and hoot'im,
And three miles off we could refute'im,
     With reasons strong,
And with false doctrines durst impute'im,
     And tenets wrong.

Then you, my young friend, must walk the round
Of scientific, college ground;
With joy of heart I always found,
     E'en after all,
Your sentiment like Peter, sound,
     Or 'postle Paul.

When in full manhood you appear,
Youth on your side, and prospects clear,
And moving in a higher sphere,
     The fair descries ye;
Kind heaven, to check some wild career,
     Points out Louisa.

Sweet heart *congenite*, heavenly fair!
She binds you in love's silken snare,
But finds herself a captive there,
     In your fond heart,
Now join'd in one united pair,
     No more to part.

Each flattering, vain, galanting rover
You scorn'd, but own'd yourself a lover;
Then sought and found me mowing clover –
     With heart full throbbing,
And all your passion did discover
     To uncle Robin.

Some loving letter to explore,
Perhaps you stopp'd a pace before,
But stumps and hillocks blundering o'er.
    I'd almost hit you –
I've wonder'd twenty times or more,
    I did not cut you.

Hail virtuous love! delightful theme,
That warms my heart with heavenly flame! –
Then turning, to the house we came,
    Well pleas'd and jolly,
And there expatiate on the same,
    With kind aunt Polly.

But what is this obscures my sight –
A cloud almost as dark as night,
That hides those darling prospects bright?
    Ah! mournful story!
Here, *Ichabod* my hand must write –
    Departed glory!

When faith's alive, my sorrow dies –
Polly still lives beyond the skies;
Christ's voice shall make her body rise
    In glory bright –
I hope to see her with these eyes,
    In robes of light.

Here cease my muse – farewell my friend;
May peace and love your life attend;
If I forget thee till mine end,
    While blood keeps running,
Or favours slight, let my right hand
    Forget her cunning.

WINDHAM, *September 5*, 1809.

To Mrs Agnes Park, On Receiving From Her A Copy Of "Waverly"

Dear madam, deign the muse to hear,
Though sounds uncouth may grate your ear,
And let rusticity appear,
    Devoid of art;
Then gratitude shall flow sincere,
    Warm from the heart.

Thanks to that generous heart of thine,
Which made that charming volume mine,
Where Highland honor, drawn so fine,
    Our hearts improve;
That doth in gallant actions shine,
    Or feats of love.

Through all intelligent creation,
The savage tribe, or polish'd nation,
In every age, or place, or station,
    Or weak, or strong,
They differ just by education
    'Bout right and wrong.

Something like virtue's found in all,
And what some may religion call,
Which infinitely short may fall –
    But what the matter?
Few stripes they'll get, or none at all,
    That know no better.

The highest pedigree I plead –
A Yankee born – true Scottish breed,
Sprung from the *Laird of Achenmead* –
    His name, *Dinsmoor*,
Who dwelt upon the banks of Tweed,
    In days of yore.

Let us that Providence adore,
Though loud Atlantic billows roar,
Which took our sires from Albion's shore,
    Or Scotia's strand,
And brought their offspring safely o'er
    To this bless'd land.

Farewell, my friend – my song must cease;
Long may you live in health and ease;
May no fell demon spoil your peace,
    With sighs and sobbing;
And while you shall remain my neice,
    I'm uncle Robin.

To Silas Betton

Dear Sir:
I sincerely sympathize with you, in your present trouble, and cannot but seriously remark the extraordinary dispensation of Divine Providence, in calling away, almost at the same time, two of your beloved nephews, whose natural talents bade fair to be useful in the world. And when I look upon the bereaved house of my late respected uncle Robin, and see, in all its branches, their wives widows, and their children fatherless, and your sister standing on the middle stage between the *aged* and the *young*, and *they* all leaning as it were upon *her*, the warm tear of pity rolls down my cheek, and my heart crys, Ah, Lord! – You will excuse me at present, and let me associated my tears with *hers*.

I am, with strong affection,
Your friend,

ROBERT DINSMOOR.

WINDHAM, *December* 19, 1809.

NOTE – The two nephews were, James Betton, who died, December 17th, aged 20 years, 9 months; and R.B. Dinsmoor, who died about the same time.

Silas Betton To Robert Dinsmoor

MY FRIEND:
I received your very friendly and sympathetic letter of the 19th instant, in due season. Indeed, it came in a time when I was peculiarly fitted to receive it. This extraordinary dispensation of Providence came near to me. – In one instance, it was like taking one of my own family. My brother and sister, on their dying bed, gave the care of their orphans to me. It was a heartfelt care, and however short I may have fallen, or come, from my duty to them, I am not conscious to myself, that in my situation I could have done more. Both orphans were equally dear to me, and to my family. One is taken, and but one left. There is, however, a pleasure in grief. I have had feelings on the occasion, I would not part with for worlds. To say nothing of the living one, few young men, deprived of parental anxiety, aid and instruction, have supported a better character than poor James. – He had no enemies. I think my own children have been benefited from the amiableness and goodness of his disposition and manners. He is removed from them, and they lament him as a brother; and it is to me heart-rending to see them cling to the survivor with double affection. I have not only had the care of their education, but of their property, for more than nineteen years. I settled with Ninian Clark Betton, when he arrived at the age of twenty-one years, in less than half an hour, for his part of his father's estate, and have several letters from him expressive of his gratitude to me for my care of his person and property. And yesterday I settled with him for James's part in as short a time. Indeed he gave me and the family much more than I charged him. Guardians are generally censured, whether they deserve it or not; but I have the peculiar pleasure of having given entire satisfaction. – They were both manly noble fellows.

In the other instance, the dispensation of Divine Providence came near to me. – My sister Ruth was my favorite. I can remember when I loved her more than any of the family. I am still fond of her. The peculiar situation in which she has stood, and now stands, has been distressing to me. I regard her children for their father's sake. I have lost many near and dear friends; but I never lost one for whom I was more distressed than for Captain Dinsmoor. The distressed situation of his family might have made it so. Besides that, he was a man of pure, unsullied integrity – placid and amiable in his manners, and I have no hesitation in saying, I thought of him as free from any guile as any man on earth. I have often thought of writing something to his memory. I have attempted it; but have always found myself too much interested and totally unable for the task. – Your native talents might do something.

SALEM, *December 22*, 1809.

Robert Dinsmoor To Silas Betton

MY WORTHY FRIEND:
I am much indebted to you for the pains you have taken to correct "Skip's Last Advice." For whether your amendment be correct or not, I am certain my honor was your motive, that the piece might appear more grammatical. Let not the insignificant term "mool," distress you – it passes very well. Mr Allen told me the other day, the poem was well received in Haverhill, and much applauded amongst his readers, as far as he could learn. I think, myself, "mools" has no singular other than *ashes*. But this is not discerned by the generality of our Scotch readers. They consider it to mean the same as *moul*, which is pretty generally understood *earth*, or *mould*; perhaps originating from *moulder*, as a body mouldering in the dust, and properly "gawin' to the mools". I some doubt whether it would stand the criticism of John Orr, Esq. or some of his sons, or perhaps a M'Keen or a M'Gregore. I am told that Capt. Hunter's wife (a M'Gregore) is the best Scotch dictionary in Londonderry, and reads it the best. Perhaps it may never reach her or them, and if it should, they make but a few of the vast number to whom Skip has addressed himself.

My dear Sir, I read with peculiar satisfaction the contents of your letter of the 22d instant. I am happy to find that you have experienced great consolation amid a scene of sorrow. The tender and impressive manner in which your brother's orphan sons were committed to your care must make them dear to you, and when you describe their characters, and in particular, the pleasing manners, life and death of the one now deceased, it excites in my breast emotions of both joy and sorrow. Your care of him is forever at an end! and although you have made a final settlement with the surviving young man, respecting the property which belonged to them, in a manner honorable both to him and you, yet I hope will still feel it to be your duty to aid him with fatherly advice and counsel, which doubtless he may yet need, and I hope he will be ever disposed to receive it form you with filial gratitude. When you speak of the distressed situation of your favorite sister, her family, her family and late husband, you touch me on a tender part. My heart bleeds at the recollection of scenes which I have witnessed in that house. Captain Dinsmoor, from his infancy, was a special friend to me. I have had many tokens of his esteem. I shall here relate one circumstance as a proof of his love. He knew the affection I had for my dear wife now dead, and he felt for me when she was sick. – A few evenings before her departure, he came to see her, and privately put a thirty dollar bill into my hands, saying, "Robin, if you stand in need, use that freely." It was a great kindness to me at that time, and I hope never to forget it. Fortunately, by the sale of a boat load of wood at Newbury, I was enabled to return it to him the next fall. He would take no interest for it, but my thanks, and that I forced upon him.

No man has a higher veneration for his memory than I have; but to write any thing on it, I feel myself entirely incompetent. But this I have said, and will say, he was a perfect pattern of honesty, frugality and industry, peaceable and kind. He was upright, honorable and manly, possessing unsullied integrity and Christian-like benevolence.

WINDHAM, *December 25*, 1809.

A Poetical Letter Addressed To Mr Allen, Printer And Editor Of The Merrimack Intelligencer

DEAR MR. ALLEN, honest printer,
When Sol moves southward of our center,
And sets us on the verge of winter,
    Stern frost before us;
We take the field, and trembling venture
    To combat Boreas.

For such conflict, 'tis best we should
Be furnish'd well with clothes and food;
Deprived of those, none e'er withstood
    A foe so cruel;
Then, meet his rage with good oak wood –
    'Tis federal fuel.

I send you, sir, a solid load
As e'er in cart or waggon rode,
Full cord-wood length, well trimm'd and stow'd
    For cheat I shall not;
Hard yellow oak, not crook'd nor bow'd,
    Chink'd up with walnut.

Not democratic smoking trash,
Like bass-wood, poplar, birch, or ash,
Built up as hollow as a squash,
    With concave top,
Where stalks for fodder in they dash,
    To fill it up.

Accept it from a rustic bard;
'Tis honestly your just reward;
Three dollars, sir, you may afford
    To give me credit –
Then I'll not fear a bailiff hoard,
    I've sometime dreaded.

O! may you never need to doom
Your lady fair, in beauty's bloom,
To shiver in a chilly room!
    This would distress you.
When federal wood dispels the gloom,
    Her smiles will bless you.

In days when nations, great and wise,
Pretend to friendship in disguise;
When ministers are charged with lies,
    To please the faction,
And Gallic scribblers dare despise
    And rail at Jackson.

Be fearless, just, and "not too rash;"
Then may your patrons pay their cash;
Those fiends, whose creeds and practice clash,
    May you discern them,
And with discretion deal the lash,
    And better learn them.

May the Intelligencer's page
Be ever useful to this age,
And ever free from party rage,
    May it abide;
And o'er your press and person sage,
    Wisdom preside.

WINDHAM, *December 1*, 1809.

Samuel Armor To Robert Dinsmoor

WINDHAM, *Feb.* 10, 1810.

SIR – Within a few days, I accidentally came across the following Fable, (altered from Gay, to illustrate the doctrine of insinuating insults by implication) and knowing you not only to be a friend to the muses, but a judge of poetical merit, I transcribe the same, and have taken the liberty to send it to you, for your personal perusal, not doubting that you will be pleased with it.

> I KNOW you ministers can with ease,
> Twist words and meanings as you please;
> That language by your skill made pliant,
> Will bend to favor all you'd spy in't;
> That 'tis the wish directs the sense,
> To make our e'en your side's pretence.
> Since things are thus, *se defendo*,
> I bar fallacious inuendo.
> If I lash vice in general fiction,
> Do I apply, or self conviction?
> Brutes are my them. – Am I to blame
> If men in morals are the same?
> I no man call an ape or ass;
> 'Tis his own conscience holds the glass.
> Thus, void of all offence I write –
> Who claims the fable knows his right.

> A shepherd's dog, unskill'd in sports,
> Pick'd up acquaintance of all sorts;
> Among the rest, a fox he knew;
> By frequent chat their friendship grew –
> As on a time the fox held forth,
> On conscience, honesty, and worth,
> Sudden he stopp'd – he cock'd his ear;
> Low dropt his brushy tail with fear; –

What's all that clatter on the road?
Bless us, the hunters are abroad;
Hold, says the dog, we're safe from harm –
'Twas nothing but a false alarm.
At yonder town 'tis market day;
Some farmer's wife is on the way –
'Tis so; I know her pyebald mare;
She's bringing forth her poultry ware.
Reynard grew huff. Says he, this sneer,
From you, I little thought to hear;
Your meaning in your looks I see;
Say! what's dame Dobbin's friend to me?
Did I e'er make her poultry thinner?
Prove that I owe the dame a dinner.
Friend, qouth the cur, I meant no harm,
Then why so captious? why so warm?
My words, in common acceptation.
Could never give this provovation.
No lamb (for aught I ever knew)
May be more innocent than you.
At this gall'd Reynard winc'd and swore
Such language ne'er was given before.
What's lamb to me? This saucy hint
Shows me, base knave, which way you squint.
If th' other night your master lost
Three lambs, am I to pay the cost?
Your vile reflections would imply
That I'm the thief! – You dog, you lie!
Thou knave, thou fool, the dog replied,
The name is just, take either side;
Thy guilt these applications speak.
Sirrah! 'Tis conscience makes you squeak.
So saying, on the fox he flies –
The self-convicted felon dies.

Robert Dinsmoor To Samuel Armor

WINDHAM, *February,* 21, 1810.

DEAR SIR – Your parabolical and truly poetical Fable, I think discovers marks of high ingenuity in its author, and is one of the best satires on the late policy of our national government, of any thing I have yet seen, and with pleasure I contribute my mite in praise of its merit.

With pleasure, sir, I must confess,
I read your friendly short address.
The compliment on me conferr'd;
I should be proud of, if deserv'd;
I own the muse's potent charms,
Her genial flame my bosom warms.
Though at her shrine I sometimes bow,
Idolatry I diasavow.
To rightly judge poetic merit,
But few the talent doth inherit;
And to impute that gift to me,
Must border, sir, on flattery;
But since the wish directs the sense,
Be sure your friend takes no offence,
Though vanity be raised no matter,
I'll not believe you meant to flatter,
Your well-wrought fable I've perused,
And o'er the curious pictures mused;
And by the portraits I could see,
Were never meant such curs as me,
Perhaps they're found among the great,
No less than ministers of state!
For oh! this truth may be lamented,
Men oft by brutes are represented!
That some are dogs, we must not say,
Although in morals base as they;
Yet bards inspired, with safety can

Make dog, or fox, to ape a man;
And by a pyebald mare, or nag,
Present to view the Gallic flag –
Make the false fox, from conscious guilt,
Charge shepherd's dog with grand insult;
And make the rascal so behave,
As show himself both fool and knave –
Make surly mastiff gape and growl.
And fright poor Reynard to the soul;
And name them, just as we do oxen –
Cal Reynard, *Smith* – the Bull-Dog, *Jackson*!

Lines Addressed To Lt. David Gregg, On The Return Of The Soldiers From Bennington Battle, Sept, 26, 1777

ON every side I hear a cheerful sound,
Gladness and mirth this morning doth abound –
I'll run and see what all this noise doth mean,
Among the crowd that stand upon the green;
But suddenly I'm struck with sweet surprise,
For welcome, welcome, welcome! each one cries,
And Windham's heroes in the midst I see,
And hear a friend's inquiring after me.
I see the fathers welcome home their boys,
Their quivering speech fulfills each other's joys,
Here comes a mother to embrace her sons,
But can't contain, and from their presence runs.
And loving brothers here again do meet,
With compliments of friendship, others greet;
Here sweetest nymphs come in with gentle pace,
But generous love beguiles the fairest face.
Those youths in raptures, urged by love's command,
Do meet the fair, and take them by the hand,
While tears of joy do wash their ruddy cheeks,
Which their fond hearts' sweet feeling plainly speaks,
And to improve a moment of such bliss,
They seal their joys all in one balmy kiss.
Old Windham rears her venerable head,
Wak'd with the news that makes her daughters glad.
She sees her sons, and thus she does impart.
The joy and fondness of her noble heart.
Hail, martial sons, who dread no dire alarms!
Welcome once more – you're welcome to my arms!
You, to defend me, took the hostile field,
And bravely did compel the foe to yield.
At your return, my spirits do rejoice,
My daughters, too, shall raise each lovely voice,

And from each lofty hill, and verdant plain,
Sing, welcome home, to each victorious swain;
And Jenny's Hill shall sound your lasting fame,
Till Cobbet's pond re-echoes back the same.

Lines, Wherein Young Jonney Praises His Cousin Molly

Yestre'en I heard young Jonney say,
"O ! but I lang to see the day,
That cousin Mally I may hae,
    To be my wife –
That I might freely wi' her liv'
    E'en a' my life.

She is a bonny lass indeed,
An's come o' a right honest breed,
An' weel she can baith write an' read,
    An' speaks right swash –
To get her aff, there'll be nae need
    To gie much cash.

Whene'er she enters in my sight,
Her very presence gi'es delight,
For ilka thing 'bout her is right,
    Her hair sae snod is –
Her shapes by day, her words by night,
    Prove her a goddess.

She is right canny at her wark,
An' thinks but little o' a daurk –
At making hats o' smooth birch-bark,
    I'm sure she dings –
She, brisk and bonny as a lark,
    Melodious sings.

Robert Dinsmoor To Silas Betton

WINDHAM, *February*, 26, 1811.

SIR – The following verses, which I here address to you, as my peculiar friend, were written on account of your requesting me to write some lines for the anniversary of the new year. If I know any thing of the poet, he must write as he feels, or not at all. The late bereavement which I have experienced, in the loss of a beloved daughter, occasioned me to reflect on other past scenes, which turned my mind rather upon the melancholy, and the plaintive is not my natural strain. I had thoughts of never shewing them to any body; but am confident you will never expose them to my hurt. I have entitled it "The Poet's Farewell to the Muses."

The Poet's Farewell To The Muses

I.

FORBEAR, my friend, withdraw your plea,
Ask not a song from one like me,
  O'ercast with clouds of sorrow!
My spring of life, and summer's fled,
I mourn those darling comforts dead,
  Regardless of tomorrow!
My harp is on the willow hung,
  Nor dissipated the gloom!
My sweetest minstrel's all unstrung,
  And silent as the tomb!
    My lute too, is mute too,
    While drops the trickling tear!
    My organ makes jargon,
    And grates my wounded ear.

II.

Farewell, yon mould'ring mansion, there,
Where first I drew the natal air,
  And learn'd to prate and play
There rose a little filial band
Beneath kind parents' fostering hand –
  Their names let live for aye!
They taught their offsprind there to read
  And hymn their Maker's praise,
To say their catechism and creed,
  And shun their vicious ways,
    They careful and prayerful
    Their pious precepts press'd,
    With ample example
    Their children still were bless'd.

III.

Kind man! my guardian and my sire,
Friend of the muse and poet's lyre,
  With genuine wit and glee,
How sweetly did his numbers glide,
When all delighted by his side,
  He read his verse to me!
The parallel was drawn between
  The freedom we possess'd,
And where our fathers long had been
  By lords and bishops press'd.
  His rhyme then did chime then,
  Like music through my heart;
  Desiring, aspiring,
  I strove to gain his art.

IV.

No more I'll tune the poet's lyre,
No more I'll ask the muse's fire,
  To warm my chilling breast;
No more I'll feel the genial flame,
Nor seek a poet's deathless fame,
  But silent sink to rest.
Farewell, the mount, call'd Jenny's Hill –
  Ye stately oaks and pines!
Farewell, you pretty purling rill,
  Which from its brow declines,
  Meandering and wandering
  The woodbines sweet among,
  Where pleasure could measure
  The bobylinkorn's song!

V.

On summer evenings, calm and bright,
O'er yonder summit's towering height,
  With pleasure did I roam;
Perhaps to seek the robin's young,

Or hear the mavis' warbling tongue,
   And bring the heifer's home –
See from my foot, the night-hawk rise,
   And leave her unfledged pair,
Then quick descending from the skies,
   Like lightning cut the air.
   The hares there, she scares there,
     And through the pines they trip,
   They're sought then, and caught then,
     By my companion, Skip.

VI.

Andover's steeples there were seen,
While o'er the vast expanse between,
   I did with wonder gaze;
There, as it were beneath my feet,
I view'd my father's pleasant seat –
   My joy in younger days.
There Windham Range, in flowery vest,
   Was seen in robes of green,
While Cobbet's Pond, from east to west,
   Spread her bright waves between.
   Cows lowing, cocks crowing,
     While frogs on Cobbet's shore,
   Lay croaking and mocking
     The bull's tremendous roar.

VII.

The fields no more their glories wear,
The forest now stand bleak and bare,
   All of their foliage stript;
The rosy lawn, the flowery mead,
Where lambkins used to play and feed,
   By icy fingers nipt.
No more I'll hear with ravish'd ears,
   The music of the wood,
Sweet scenes of youth, now gone with years
   Long pass'd beyond the flood.

Bereav'd and grieved,
I solitary wail,
With sighing and crying,
My drooping spirits fail.

VIII.

No more will I the Spring Brook trace.
No more with sorrow view the place
   Where Mary's wash-tub stood,
No more I'll wander there alone,
And lean upon the mossy stone,
   Where once she pil'd her wood.
'Twas there she bleach'd her linen cloth,
   By yonder bass-wood tree;
From that sweet stream she made her broth,
   Her pudding and her tea,
    Whose rumbling and tumbling
   O'er rocks with quick dispatch,
    Made ringing and singing,
   None but her voice could match.

IX.

Farewell, sweet scenes of rural life,
My faithful friends and loving wife,
   But transient blessings all.
Bereft of those I sit and mourn;
The spring of life will ne'er return,
   Chill death grasps great and small;
I fall before thee, God of truth!
   O, hear my prayer and cry;
Let me enjoy immortal youth,
   With saints above the sky.
    Thy praise there, I'll raise there,
   With all my heart and soul,
    Where pleasure and treasure,
   In boundless oceans roll.

Notes.

My dear friend, lest you should not be able to understand my poem in some particulars, I shall here make a few explanatory notes.

VERSE 1. – In this you will easily understand scenes of sorrow through which I have recently passed, and that I am now in the decline of life, and bereft of some, and must soon bid adieu to all, those sweet voices that once charmed me.

VERSE 2. – *"My sweetest minstrel" &c.* This refers to the place of my nativity, my father's old mansion house, part of which is now a ruinous heap, and to those scenes of childhood and youth, which I passed with my brothers and sisters, under the instruction of our venerable parents.

VERSE 3. – This is wholly devoted to my father's memory and honor, and I desire never to die until I do some justice to his name. He was certainly the man I there describe.

"The parallel was drawn between the freedom we possess'd"
 This alludes to a poetic epistle which he wrote to John Dinsmoor, of Ireland, a kinsman of his, to encourage him to come with his family to this country, in the year 1766. The original, and many other pieces which might have done honor to his memory, were destroyed by the mice, in his little repository, some years before his death. I know not that any part of the poem is remembered by a soul on earth except the little that still rests on my memory; and here I give it to you:

> "The parallel is not right drawn,
> Ye will be apt to say,
> Ye tell the worst side o' our lan',
> On yours, the best, ye may.
> I own yours is a pleasant lan',
> But O! the rotten breath
> O' Lairds an' Bishops, Satan's ban',
> Maist poisons folk to death!
> Here fish an' fowling baith are free –

> Our waters, nane do watch them;
> All fish that swim, an' birds that flee,
> Are ours, where'er we catch them;
> Though ilka ewe *twa* lambs should bring,
> The bishops has nae gain,
> For to our joy, in ilka thing,
> The *tenth* is ay our ain."

The piece was long, but this is all I retain of it. I have here said a good deal of my father; but lest I should never have an opportunity to speak or write of him again, let this be his epitaph by me:

> *Peace to his ashes – let him rest!*
> *He ne'er was found below man*
> *True honest virtue fill'd his breast –*
> *He was a foe to no man.*

VERSE 4. – *"The mound call'd Jenny's Hill."*

On this hill stood my father's house. It derived its name from Jane M'Gregore, daughter of the first minister of Londonderry, to whom he bequeathed it, containing about three hundred acres. It has since obtained the name of *Dinsmoor's Hill*.

VERSE 5, and 6, relates to the pleasing prospects which in summer may be seen from that beautiful eminence. I long and hope yet to have an opportunity of traveling up this little *Parnassus* with some and some other of my friends.

VERSE 7, and 8, will need little explanation. You will see they relate principally to my local situation, and various circumstances and things, which are not unknown to you that have attended to it. "The Spring Brook," is that small stream that crosses the road a little east of my house. The fountain, from which it issues, supplies my aqueduct, and in the days of the dear woman here alluded to, came into my house.

DEAR SIR – Since I wrote the preceding notes, I have been at Captain Robert Nesmith's in Londonderry, and, conversing freely about our parents, I asked him if there were any of my father's old letters in being, which he sent to his mother, (my father's sister) who was enthusiastically fond of his poetry. He said he had, not long since, seen a large bundle of them, and he believed they were gone to Daniel Anderson's, with his mother's chest. He showed me one humorous piece, which he had recorded in his copy-book, which he promised to transcribe for me, and another little billet inviting his father and mother to a *blyth-meet*, as our old people used to call it, which I here give you, without altering its diction.

WINDHAM, *May* 21, 1774.

Dear brither, pardon, if I at this time,
Should twa'r three words put into broken rhyme.
'Tis said, frae kings we may ask what we want,
Yet they're na forc'd a' that we ask to grant.
Do ye na think, 'twad heartless be indeed,
If to our prayers they never wad gie heed?
I ken wi' me ye'll join, an' answer, yes –
Permit me, then, lest I my mark may miss,
To beg you'd not reject my humble prayer,
But come an' see us, We'n'sday o' the fair.
I think poor farmers very justly may,
When planting's done, tak' twa'r three days o' play.
Bring Mally wi' ye, an' be sure yese get
A hearty welcome baith frae me an' Bet.
At ony time, if ever ye demand
The like frae me, I'll pay it – here's my hand:
The sun about the globe has six times run,
Since Bess, my kimmer, brought me hame a son;
Come, then, awa', let's ither's faces see –
Until that time, ye's hear nae mair frae me.

From yer brither,

BILLY DINSMOOR

To MR. JAMES NESMITH

Robert Dinsmoor To Silas Betton

DEAR SIR:
I HAVE herewith sent you "Spring's Lamentation and Confession," which you will find inscribed to you. This poem may appear satirical, and in some measure severe; but you will pardon the muse when I give you the following information:

This little dog had lived some years in my father's family before his decease; and in the provision which he made for my mother, which was ample, she was left sole proprietor of all his buildings and stock. Soon after this period my youngest sister was married, and moved away; and William (who in the poem is called Billy) only, of all her numerous children remained in her family. About this time, William was engaged in building his new house, and occasionally often from home. The good old lady was many times left without any company but her little dog. In the course of about two years he took possession of his new house, and persuaded my mother to come and keep it for him. This she consented to do rather than repair the old one, which was much decayed. But here Billy soon left her, and to make a spec, let out his farm, and went to Charlestown, and let himself to a shipbuilder, where he continued four years. During this time she made Billy's new house her habitation; but her heart was still in the old-mansion house. She paid it frequent visits, and always in summer occupied her old bleaching green at the back of it. Spring never failed to attend her. All the brute creatures that my father left with her, were either sold, changed, or dead, except the mare and the dog. In this solitary state, her attachment seemed to increase towards those two animals, in the absence of her other friends. Spring was always subject to err; but his mistress could always forgive him, judging, as everyone must, who knew the little cur, that it proceeded more from want of thought, than a design to injure. He was her company both by night and day, and the mare was her pleasure carriage when she chose to ride out. The mare is still alive, and the old lady is yet able to ride her, and does so frequently to your little city, and Haverhill town, and does her own business, although at the advanced age of seventy six. Billy at length returned, and had longed to smoke a long pipe like other fashionable young gentlemen. He then painted up his house in style and soon got married. Spring was amazing fond of his old friend, and would follow him almost every where he went, and especially to meeting, which practice Billy utterly abhorred; he used to shut him up on Lord's days at home; but Spring generally made his way out, and if the doors were shut when he got to meeting, he would yell and tear more like a fiend than a dog. But he soon found that this stratagem would answer his purpose; for Deacon Morrison would let him in rather than suffer his noise. But one day, taking the start of the Deacon, Billy outwitted him, and just as he entered the door, Billy grabbed him by the tail and gave him a most unmerciful whipping. In the course of a few days, some *tattling tell-tale* brought the whole affair to the old lady's ears; and a strong jealousy instantly arose in her mind, that Spring suffered more for abusing Billy's new house than for disturbing the congregation; and calling Billy to her apartment, she said, "There, take and kill the dog outright, for he shall not live to be abused." He absolutely refused to do it, and I know he would almost as soon as committed parricide, as have killed or destroyed any thing in which she seemed to take comfort. John A********, David's son, was then making shoes at my house, and she remembered with what pleasure he used to kill her supernumerary cats, and came stepping down and invited him to come up in the evening and bring Robin's Billy with him, and kill her dog; with all cheerfulness he promised to oblige her. Notwithstanding my pointed disapprobation, he completed the tragedy in the evening. I then "the muse unfetter'd, and gave her play." Probably you may wish to know who the other personages are, mentioned in this poem.

"When Nabby's Sunday clothes," &c. – A young woman, learning to be a Tailoress with my brother William's wife, with whom Spring had scraped up an intimate acquaintance. In the old lady's last address to Spring, she expresses herself,

"O' a' the beasts that Father left." – This was the endearing name by which the humble old lady for many years called her husband, and she yet speaks of him in the same manner.

"Auld John"—mentioned in the last line of the poem, was our shoemaker's own Uncle, and something of a professional man.

"*Then I set off for Jonny's house,*" – My brother John, the blacksmith, where Spring, was peculiarly familiar.

I tried to make the little rascal speak English at first, but I soon found he was far better versed in Scotch. He was both illiterate and vulgar, and his lingo will yet admit of many corrections.

I am, Sir, with great respect,
Your sincere friend,

ROBERT DINSMOOR.

Spring's Lamentation And Confession
INSCRIBED TO SILAS BETTON, ESQ.

> *Some rhyme, a neebor's name to lash;*
> *Some rhyme, (vain thought) for needfu' cash;*
> *Some rhyme to court the countra clash,*
>   *An' raise a din;*
> *For me, an aim I never fash –*
>   *I rhyme for fun.*
>   BURNS.

Alas! An' I'm condemn'd to death!
A Cobler now maun stap my breath;
To lea' my Dame, I'm very laith,
    Though 'tis her sentence;
May he that caus'd it, an' she baith,
    Soon get repentance.

Lang hae I liv'd we' kind Miss Bessy,
Wha kept me cozie, warm an' fleshy;
In lanely hours she would caress me,
    An' mak' me fain,
Baith e'en and morn I gat a messy,
    As though her wean.

Where'er she travel'd night or day,
I carefu' was to clear her way
O' toads an' snakes, and I maun say,
    I've shaw'd my spunk;
For though I never dar'd to *slay*,
    I've *scar'd* – a skunk.

If she walk'd out when days were hot,
Sometimes before her I wad trot,
An' mony a fright wi' me she's got,
    For in a trice,

I'd gie a spring as quick as shot,
    An' bark at mice.

Nor yet was this my only fault.
Though I maun *die* I'll own my guilt;
When clos'd within they bade me halt
    On Sabbath day,
My teeth hath doors an' windows spoilt,
    An' ope'd my way.

A'e day I left my dame in lurch,
An' after Billy trudg'd to church;
An' neither dreading whip or birch,
    Wi' teeth an' paw,
An' hedious yells at the west porch,
    I 'gan to gnaw.

The very priest was scar'd himsel',
His sermon he could hardly spell;
Auld Carlins fancied they could smell,
    The brimstone matches;
They thought I was some imp o' hell,
    In quest o' wretches.

Then Billy grasp'd a lang whip stick,
An' stept towards me wondrous quick;
Quoth I, "he's coming in the nick,
    Hear how he hurries on –
Sure 'tis another kindly trick
    Of Elder Morrison."

As soon's I heard the moving latch,
I press'd my head in, silly wretch!
But ah! waes me! I found my match;
    For by my tail,
Bill wi' a strong grip did me catch,
    And did me whail.

All sorts o' murder I cri'd out,
While Billy swung me roun' about,
And thresh'd my sides, an' back, an' snout,
  An' coust me by,
Baith priest an' parish thought nae doubt,
  I dead did lie.

My last an' warst fau't here I'll tell on,
For which I'm dying like a felon;
When Nabby's Sunday clothes were well on,
  She lock'd me in;
Her tracks I almost swore I'd smell on,
  O, horrid sin!

In painted room where I was pent,
(To win without was my intent;
Lest Nabby's tracks should lose the scent,)
  I tore the sash,
Bill's lang pipe frae the window went,
  An' brak' to smash.

I hope to catch the bonnie lass,
I stove my head right through the glass;
But something that sharp pointed was,
  My side did bore,
And frae my shouther to my base,
  My hide it tore.

For speed o' foot but few could stan' her,
Tho' in a bicker I've out ran her;
But 'mang the crowd, I did na' ken her,
  (Poor silly stirk,)
'Till snoaking roun' at length I foun' her,
  Snug in the kirk.

For this my dame wi' aching side,
Did a' the way to Hav'rill ride;
And laid a dollar out beside,
  Glass pipe an' putty –

My very conscience canna' bide
    Those actions smutty.

My mistress cri'd, "Poor Spring come till me,
This night (she said) the boys will kill ye;
This shoemaker and Robin's Billy,
    Will soon be here –
I'd just as lief, I am sae silly,
    They'd fell the meare.

O' a' the beasts that Father left,
You and the meare are just the heft;
The sentence past I maunna shift –
    How can I bear
To be at ance o' you bereft" –
    An' drapt a tear.

" 'Twas na' because I loe'd you neither,
That we hae liv'd sae kind the gether,
But for the love I bore to father,
    Wha's beast ye were,
Frae that sprang a' my kindness rather,
    An' a' my care.

It's true *my* days are almost gone,
I find old age fast creeping on;
My comforts fail me every one,
    So, Spring, adieu –
I've something else to think upon,
    Than things like you."

My woe, quoth I, seize th' Armstrong chiel,
I dread him like the very de'el,
Ay since his shoe-knife gart me feel,
    The pains o' death –
Oh! loch! how I did growl an' squeel,
    To say my graith.

Then aff I set for Jonny's house;
The Armstrong cobler me pursues,
An' roun' my neck he fixt a noose,
  Wi' girnin' laugh –
And snak'd me out as auld John us'd
  To draw a calf!

Robert Dinsmoor To Silas Betton

WINDHAM, *September* 28, 1812.

MY DEAR SIR – I take the liberty to address the following poems to you, and wish you to correct it and send me you candid remarks upon it. I will not say criticism, lest it should prevent my ever writing any more. It was occasioned by my crushing a nest of Sparrow's eggs, when I was ploughing among the corn, July 20, 1812. And about that time, I saw a well done piece in the Haverhill Intelligencer, in imitation of Burn's delightful Nanny, which induced me to adopt the Scottish dialect, that it might the better resemble his beautiful mountain daisy.—I call it *The Sparrow*.

The Sparrow

Poor innocent and hapless Sparrow!
Why should my moul-board gie thee sorrow?
This day thou'll chirp, an' mounr the morrow,
    Wi' anxious breast –
The plough has turn'd the mould'ring furrow
    Deep o'er thy nest.

Just in the middle o' the hill,
Thy nest was plac'd wi' curious skill;
There I espy'd thy little bill
    Beneath the shade –
In that sweet bower secure frae ill,
    Thine eggs were laid.

Five corns o' maize had there been drappit,
An' through the stalks thine head, thou pappit;
The drawing nowt couldna' be stappit,
    I quickly foun' –
Syne frae thy cozie nest thou happit,
    An' flutt'ring ran.

The sklentin stane beguil'd the sheer,
In vain I tri'd the plough to steer;
A wee bit stumpie i' the reaer,
    Cam' 'tween my legs –
An' to the jee side gart me veer,
    An' crush thine egges.

Alas! alas! my bonnie birdie!
Thy faithfu' mate flits roun' to guard ye.
Connubial love ! a pattern wordy
    The pious priest!
What savage heart could be sae hardy,
    As wound thy breast?

Thy ruin was nae fau't o' mine,
(It gars me greet to see thee pine;)
It may be serves his great design,
    Who governs all;
Omniscience tents wi' eyes divine,
    The Sparrow's fall.

A pair more friendly ne'er were married,
Their joys an' pains were equal carried;
But now, ah me! to grief they're hurried,
    Without remead;
When all their hope an' treasure's buried.
    'Tis sad indeed.

How much like theirs are human dools!
Their sweet wee bairns laid I' the mools,
That sovereign Pow'r who nature rules,
    Has said so be it;
But poor blin' mortals are sic' fools,
    They canna' see it.

Nae doubt, that He wha' first did mate us,
Has fixt our lot as sure as fate is,
And when he wounds, he disna' hate us,
    But only this –
He'll gar the ills that here await us,
    Yield lasting bliss.

A Father's Lament
For The Death Of A Favourite Daughter

Why, O my soul, this sad complaint?
Why should my groans my sorrows vent?
Why flow these tears without restraint
    O'er Betsey's urn?
The pleasant favour Heav'n me lent,
    I must return.

When but an infant, prattling, young,
I was delighted with her tongue;
But joys extatic, when she sung,
    Charm'd all my heart;
Time shew'd her minstrel heav'nly strung,
    Improv'd by art.

Why should reflection paint her mien,
And figure, graceful to be seen;
With mind unruffled and serene,
    I envied state –
Her conscious innocence was screen,
    'Gainst causeless hate.

The heart that warm'd her lovely breast,
Could melt for those who were distess'd;
Her ready hands to help th' oppressed,
    She would employ;
When all was well, then she was blest,
    And sang for joy!

When at her wasting cough I'd start,
She well discern'd my inward smart;
"Sing, dad," she'd say, to sooth my heart,
    And cheerful smile;
And with her well-tun'd counter part,
    My griefs beguile.

No more her little sister band
Shall time their music by her hand!
No more shall she a leader stand
  Her mates among,
And pay her Maker's just demand,
  A sacred song!

When sickness press'd, or pains did bend me,
O! with what care she would attend me!
If I was straiten'd, she'd befriend me,
  With love so true,
Her hard earn'd dollar she would lend me,
  And help me through!

The prophet, shelter'd in his bower,
From scorching heat and pending shower,
Was of his hope in one short hour
  Bereft! – Ah, Lord!
E'en so, a worm destroyed my flower,
  Like Jonah's gourd!

Farewell, my sweet, my much loved Betty!
While life remains, I'll not forget thee,
Though death untimely did beset thee,
  And laid you low;
To hopeless mourn, O, never let me,
  Nor sink in wo.

Despair shall not my faith annoy,
Her soul immortal, shall not die!
Her dust shall rise, and see with joy,
  A Saviour's face,
And shall a golden harp employ
  In endless praise!

WINDHAM, *December* 10, 1810.

Letter From Robert Dinsmoor To His Daughter

WINDHAM, *February* 29, 1812.

MY DEAR SALLY – I have written so little of late, that it is with reluctance that I attempt it – nothing but the affection of my heart for you, could induce me to write as I now do. You know my passions, foibles, and failings – and I do hope, you, and all my children, have goodness enough to throw a mantle over them. I shall make no apology for the verses I send you, they come warm from my heart. Some of the ideas, I think might be improved and enlarged; but I know your sagacity, (and not to make you proud,) good judgment, and natural talents and acquirements, will enable you to catch the ideas and improve them.

Robert Dinsmoor To His Daughter Sally

THE cause is not for want of matter,
That I can't write a longer letter;
Of that there's plenty, worse of better;
    But like a mill,
Whose stream beats back with surplus water,
    My wheel stands still.

Of cares domestic, I might tell,
Or whether we are sick or well,
Or what disasters have befel
    Our friends around us;
And how with patience we dispel
    The griefs that wound us.

Tell how the tyrant death proceeds,
And how a father's bosom bleeds –
His son the staff his age now needs,
    Laid low and chilly –
Shew Peggy dress'd in mourning weeds,
    For her lov'd Billy.

Alas! poor Peggy is it so,
That you in silent mourning go,
And lonely sigh a widow's woe,
    And bear the smart?
Such pains and sorrows you must know,
    Pierc'd Jacob's heart.

Here I would ask but am afraid,
Why were two hearts congenial made?
Why beauty's charms love's passions aid,
    And rapture raise?
Yet doom'd to part in death's dark shade,
    In youth's sweet days.

Who knows what troubles some must bear?
What pains and sorrows they shall share?
What grief anxiety and care,
    E'en we shall meet,
Before we reach the mansion where,
    Bliss is complete?

Then let us knot impatient grow;
But to our lot submissive bow.
God's ways are just, we know not how;
    Bless him alway.
Hope must be all out comfort now,
    Then sing and say –

Farewell, bright souls! a short farewell,
'Till we shall meet our joys to tell,
In the sweet groves, where pleasures dwell,
    In fields above,
And trees of life, of heavenly smell,
    Bear fruits of love!

Robert Dinsmoor To Silas Betton

WINDHAM, *December* 22, 1812.

MY DEAR SIR – I send you enclosed, The Carrier of the Merrimack Intelligencer, to his patrons &c. If you think it admissible, you may present it to the Messrs. Allens. They expect something of the kind from me, and look for it through your hands.

I am persuaded that any thing that has received your sanction will be printed, "without consulting flesh and blood." I am very sure if it steps into the field in its present garb, it will be viewed as Goliath did David – and every uncircumcised democratic Anakim will curse it in the name of his gods. Therefore, I give you full liberty to point, correct, inspect, criticise, expunge and destroy, as may seem good in your sight. I put it into your hands as ore into the furnace, and wish it to be tried, as by fire. If there is gold in it, it will come out pure, but if it should prove to be all reprobate silver, let it all go to oblivion together. Consider what you have at stake, and let not the "Rustic Bard" expose himself to eternal contempt.

N.B. I have written the almost the whole piece this evening, since I came home from Haverhill with my team. As I am something sleepy, and my sight naturally bad, it is but poorly done. If I had time, or could see to take another view of it, I might perhaps correct some of it myself. It will soon be "some wee short hour ayont the twall."

The Post-Boy's Address.
*The Carrier Of The Merrimack Intelligencer
To His Patrons. January, 1813*

Of time's long annals that are past,
No year was ever like the last;
All Christendom engaged in arms,
And nothing's heard but war's alarms.
To get religion quite destroy'd,
Hell has its legions all employ'd.
I'm but a news-boy or a courier,
Yet for the times none e'er was sorrier.
You may think strange that such a dunce,
Should now turn poet all at once;
But Bards are prophets, you should know it;
King David was a royal poet,
He told the folk then things to come,
And I perhaps may tell you some. –
If Madison be re-elected,
Great troubles may be soon expected.
When in disguise a fast he calls,
"To twenty gods or none," he falls!
French influence so pervades his heart,
He's now in league with Bonaparte;
He's so allur'd with Gallic charms,
He'll fall asleep in Bona's arms.
So Sampson sweetly took a nap,
On a deceitful harlot's lap,
Nor yet Philistine lords he fears,
'Till off his hair and strength she shears.
That Madison should be compared
To Sampson, some may think it hard;
The contrast is too great that's given,
Although I'm sure he will be shaven;
And when alliance cords do bind him,
His masters then no doubt will blind him.
Alas ! it seems some Gallic lady

Has put out both his eyes already;
He can't discern a single star,
To guide his course in this dark war;
The officers he sends abroad,
Cannot command their troops a rod –
O ! tell it not in Gath to one,
Nor publish it in Askelon!
Of things that's past I'll give a sketch o' them.
Late feats of war no matter which o' them;
I burn to mention that exploit,
How Hull surrender'd Fort Detroit.
And how the Demo's all have curs'd him
Because brave General Brock did worst him –
Van Renselaer fled from the field,
And left his men to die or yield,
Pretending to get force to aid them;
But here he says they disobey'd him –
Would you hear Hopkins' expedition,
With patriots arm'd and full provision?
As mounted riflemen they were,
They thought all Canada to scare;
Six hard day's march he did pursue
That warlike tribe call'd Kickapoo;
But just before he got the sight o' them
His troops all turn'd about in spite o' him –
And as there was no foe to fear,
Their glorious leader took the rear;
Then all flew off as wild as ducks,
Pursued by nothing but the flux!
If this should seem a low idea,
Take Hopkin's words – "a diarrhœa."
What cost them six days' march 'tis true,
They all retrac'd safe back in two.
There's our great Generalissimo!
He would take Canada you know';
"A strapping lad" the ladies doat on,
Whene'er he gets his fine lace coat on –
He rode at favorite Miss's call,

Sixty miles south t'attend a ball;
But lest his laurels should be stain'd,
One grand achievement he obtain'd –
A great discovery has been made;
A reconoit'ring party said,
Close in behind a little wood,
A bold menacing block-house stood –
Then he detach'd a host off-hand,
And gave it to Chandler the command;
A minute now must not be lost,
They all with speed the river cross'd.
The dire event! they thought they'd risk it,
And took the block house and one musket!
Just so they think they'll take Quebec –
One poor man only broke his neck.
This strong hold they so fierce surrounded,
Six of their own men they were wounded!
And if the papers do not lie,
One of those wounded men did die.
Then all return'd except some martyrs,
Where Dearborn rests in winter quarters.
But who could lead like General Smyth,
His troops to conquest or to death?
His standard place with courage brave,
On great Montgomery's glorious grave?
Though our vain hero thus did boast,
He, nor his troops the river cross'd;
But thought it best to save their lives,
By running home to see their wives, –
And quitting thoughts of all invasions,
Gave Congress back their proclamations!
His soldiers now can mock and hoot at 'em,
And some have even dar'd to shoot at 'em.
So great a mountain travell'd sore,
Brought forth a mouse, and did no more!
God only knows what times will turn to,
To every nation we're a scorn to.
No facts nor reasoning can convince

Our Lilliputian pu'rile prince.
It seems to give them consolation,
To see our country's degradation;
He thinks as men and means grow scarcer,
'Twill only make them fight the fiercer.
With England he keeps up the bustle,
And goads them on by Agent Russell;
To all their force he bids defiance,
And threatens them with French alliance,
And conquests that forbid a peace,
And says that wars shall never cease.
And by his hotch-potch flimsy speech,
He'd make us think we're growing rich.
If that were true, our patrons might
Pay for their papers upon sight.
Then I with pleasure round would steer,
And carry news another year.
There's one thing more, which all now tell us,
We've yet some hardy, true, good fellows.
Both Hull and Jones, and Brave Decatur,
Do marv'lous things upon the water.
They take, and sink, and kill, like thunder;
The Britons brave, to them knock under.
The demo's say, 'twill make up any day,
For all we've lost, in taking Canada:
But here I must break off my song –
Good bye – I fear I've stay'd too long;
But I must give you one verse more,
Before I pass the outer door.
Each Christian cry – let God arise,
And save our sinking nation!
'Tis only He, can set us free
From chains and desolation.

Robert Dinsmoor To Silas Betton

WINDHAM, *September* 18, 1813.

DEAR SIR – I am now fairly taken upon surprise. Your two daughters are now here, and I feel constrained to send you something by them in return for the polite letter you sent by Maria, and the beautiful lines enclosed. I have read them often with great pleasure and attention. Many of my friends, whom I think good judges, have pronounced them highly meritorious, and it is sincerely my opinion that they are; but I think, however, that the "Rustic Bard" is too highly flattered. I shall enclose in this the Rustic Bard's answer to the anonymous address of that kind hearted young gentleman. – Had I known sooner of this opportunity, I might have had it some better done. It is really my first draft; but I know you can correct and amend. You will please to present it to my unknown friend. I send you also, a poem, the production of an aged minstrel, of the county of Hillsborough. I think it is not without merit, although I think it is too long, and that the word "band" is too often used. My worthy friend has left it wholly under my care, with liberty to shew it to my friends. Please soon to give me your remarks upon it. I shall call for it after you shall have sufficiently amused yourself with it. Your taste of poetry, and your opinion of the structure of its measures I exactly agree with, and thank you for your strictures on mine. I am pleased with your remarks.

Ninian C. Betton To Silas Betton

HANOVER, *October* 23, 1813.

DEAR SIR – The compliment paid to my hasty production was quite unexpected. I did not expect to see it in print. It does not, however, flatter my vanity, as I am well convinced it was inserted only on account of its relation to the handsome answer it drew forth; that, I am sure, was its only merit. The hope of exciting the poet of nature's school, to a new exertion of his poetic powers, has induced me to write again, and I could think of nothing more worthy than an attempt to echo his sentiments, with a trifling addition.

Echo To the Bard's Answer

DEAR Bard, dost wonder whose the heart,
That in thy griefs could take a part,
Of pains parental feel the smart?
  Then may you know,
A lonely orphan needs no art
  To picture wo.

The heart that cannot feel thy wo,
Is colder than Siberian snow,
Nor *joys* of *grief* can ever know,
  Those joys refin'd,
Which gives to souls devotion's glow,
  And raise the mind.

But the lone youth, who feels for you,
On parents dear, and brothers too,
Of death's dread spear has had to view
  The dire effect –
His lonely being tells him true,
  His friends are "wreck'd."

In fond affection for the fair,
My heart was never wanting there,
I've oft indulg'd fond hope and prayer –
  The fair are kind;
But though dame fortune seems to stare,
  I'm sure she's blind.

Though happiness in prospect lies,
And keeps our hopes still on the rise,
The more pursu'd, the more it flies,
  And ends in grief;
Yet with our hope our comfort dies –
  There's no relief.

No mortal eye can future scan,
Nor trace the destiny of man;
We cannot trace great nature's plan –
    The search is vain;
Our lives, we find, are but a span –
    Our pleasures pain.

Your closing stanza, friendly, kind,
Bespeakes the heart and soul refin'd,
And though to future we are blind,
    The present's ours;
May we in friendship solace find,
    When fortune lowers.

Your "Sparrow" ought to place your name
High on the catalogue of fame;
That pious philosophic strain
    Has fix'd your worth;
And though stern death may victory gain,
    You'll live on earth.

We mount the heights of fame by turns,
Ambition for that summit burns,
And seeks mausoleums and urns –
    You'll have your due;
Our nation boasts another "Burns,"
    Dear Bard, in you.

                                "ORPHAN."

Response To The "Echo"

DEAR friendly youth, your "Echo's" sound,
Must from my heart again rebound;
A heart that feels another wound –
    Your orphan tale!
Mine eyes in pity's tears are drown'd,
    To hear thee wail.

Poor lonely youth! but happier far
Than thousand other orphans are,
When by a most unholy war,
    Their parents bled!
They friendless every ill must bear –
    Their comforts dead.

Not so with you – no foe to fear,
Your friends and relatives are here –
An honor'd uncle, kind and near,
    Who still will prove
Your counsellor and patron dear,
    With father's love.

Let you and I no more complain –
If reason and religion reign,
Our hearts shall soon forget their pain.
    In hope of this,
Our pious friends shall live again,
    In endless bliss.

I never wish my rhymes should fail
In literary hands at all,
Nor did I think my reed so small,
    Should e'er be found
To echo back from Dartmouth's hall,
    So sweet a sound!

I ne'er indulged a hope so dear,
As that my lays should touch the ear
Of learned pupils, standing near
    (Who write by rule,)
His seat, where science has no peet,
    In Wheelock's school.

Let vain ambition never dare
To shew my rustic numbers there,
On hallow'd ground! let me beware,
    And not intrude,
Lest literature should frown and tear
    My vesture rude.

Bright son of science, rise and shine!
Your virgin muse appears divine;
You need not ask the fabled nine
    To help or aid you;
A poet's laurels shall be thine,
    In justice paid you.

And though dame fortune may seem wild,
And spurn your wishes for a while –
Hope still – she'll yet propitious smile,
    And kind, regard you;
And with some poet's favorite child,
    In love reward you.

When your capacious mind to store,
With philosophic classic lore,
On nature's boundless works you pore,
    'Till darkness veils you;
Then rise in rapture, and adore,
    When reason fails you!

Whose searchless wisdom, boundless power,
Made heaven, and earth, and every flower;
The insect flies, and seraphs tower
    T' obey his nod;

Then let the atheist's reasoning cower,
    And own a God.

'Tis true, no finite mortal can
The smallest of God's creatures scan;
Much less, his universal plan,
    Or fix'd decree;
We might as well grasp with our span,
    A boundless sea.

Great nature's volume open stands,
The wise can read it in all lands;
But Heaven has put into our hands
    ONE more divine!
Where the Creator's just commands,
    And mercies shine!

We'll with devotion read his word,
Which light, and comfort can afford,
Where faith can see a Saviour Lord,
    In heavenly rays;
Then let our hearts in sweet accord,
    Exalt his praise.

Robert Dinsmoor To Silas Betton

WINDHAM, *February* 21, 1815.

MY DEAR FRIEND:
YOUR letter of the first inst. covering N.C. Betton's letter to you, containing the Orphan's Address to the Rustic Bard, was duly received; and it was to me like pouring oil and wine into a poor dying man's wounds. 'Tis only the needy who can justly estimate a friend. How sweet is the hand that kindly administers but the smallest comfort to one in distress. To one in trouble, there is a charm in a consoling word, and the pearly tear of sympathy exceeds all price. Your letter, sir, expressing the feelings of a friend indeed. My complaint was truly distressing, and my sickness sore; but blessed be God, my heavenly Father, He held me in his right hand, while he corrected me; and my life was precious in his sight. "What shall I render to the Lord for all his gifts to me?" I think I am yet far from a well man. I have not been so well for three days past, as I was for two or three weeks before, occasioned I believe by my taking a little cold – but I hope, with prudent care, I shall yet recover a tolerable state of health. I sincerely sympathise with you in the afflicted situation of your family. Your concern for your wife and two daughters must be great. The unhappy accident which befell Mrs. B____, beside the pain she must endure, must inevitably prevent her from giving that aid to the sick, which she usually did; and I fear it will be a great disadvantage to the girls – as I think no nurse was ever like a prudent affectionate mother. It also casts a greater burden upon those that are well. You say H____ is some better than she has been, and I hope soon to hear that W____ is better likewise. It really hurt me to hear that she was confined to her chamber. "A burnt child dreads the fire." We ought ever to endeavor to be "patient in tribulation," and never to repine at the providence of God, who ever did and will do all things well. I never doubted your friendship for me, nor your desire to have me respected while I live. But here I have a more exalted token of your regard, in that you wish to perpetuate my name, and have it respected after I am dead. I wish there was one

trait in my character worthy the imitation of posterity, or worthy your pen to record. I think, sir, it would be impossible for you to make such an obscure character as mine, interesting to the public. The probability is, now, that you will outlive me; and whether I shall be called away soon or late, never let the task of writing my life, "trouble your spirit" again. My fame, though small, or name rather by your instrumentality has already gone farther than I think it ever ought to have gone. I wish my friends to remember me while I live, and when I am dead, let a silent stone be my momento. My most worthy young friend, your nephew, N.C. Betton, has written once more like himself. His strains are always pleasing, sensible, and friendly. He in my opinion, is possessed, to say the least, of a beautifully poetic genius. And I hope he will never hide such a productive talent nor let it be lost. His address to the "Rustic Bard", (save that he has been too lavish in his encomiums,) is masterly done. His introduction, and apology for not keeping up a close correspondence with me, and his reasons why it was commenced by him are truly natural, descriptive, and honorable. The address itself, though short, carries in it the principles of a large volume. In it he has said more, and to better effect, than I could say if I should write a great book.

I congratulate you, sir, in the hope of returning peace. May we never more need to use the power of the muses to rouse our sons to war; but may the sweet songs of friendship and peace, melt down the blood thirsty tyrants, who have almost brought us to ruin, and disarm them of their power, so that they shall never be able again to draw the oppressor's sword. But what think ye? Suppose a peace is ratified between this country and Great Britain, will that make us a happy people, while the government is in the hands of our present rulers? I tell you, sir, I think not. The Democrats are the same that they always were. They have the bold effrontery to tell us to our face, "Now you see that we were right, and you were wrong – you must acknowledge our rulers have done well since they have *compelled* Great Britain to make peace." But tell them, that Monroe's letter of instructions, of April 15, 1813, says "If this encroachment of Great Britain, (meaning the right of search) is not provided against, the United States have appealed to arms in vain." And then tell them, that the same

Monroe, in his letter, January 28, 1814, says, "You may omit any stipulation on the subject of impressment, if found indispensably necessary to terminate the war," and not one of them will blush!

I with this, send you a small poem, which I call "The Retrospect." You will carefully examine it, and if you think it will at all please my young friend, N.C. Betton, you may favor him with a copy of it, if it is not too much trouble. In looking over my papers, I found a few lines to W____, written some time last May, in answer to a beautiful complimentary letter from her to me, which I venture also to enclose. Although I never thought them worth sending, yet if she is not too sick, they may perhaps divert her a little. You must judge whether she shall see them or not.

Retrospect After A Fit Of Severe Sickness

When down the stream of life we float,
As in some sinking leaky boat,
We're dash'd on shoals and rocks remote,
    Half drown'd already;
Then haply rest our way, to note,
    In some kind eddy.

Soon rushing freshets raise the flood,
Again before the storm we scud,
'Till on some craggy point we thud –
    By tempests carried;
Or in some creek stuck fast in mud,
    In waves we're buried.

Of, if perchance we keep the current,
And ride upon the foaming torrent,
We drive elate without a warrant,
    Far from the coast;
'Till plung'd beneath the wave abhorrent,
    We're sunk and lost.

So o'er the rapids I've been driven,
With wind and tide I hard have striven,
Bereft of every hope but Heaven,
    I cried distress'd;
Yet I have found some respite given,
    To breath and rest.

When bilious pains did sore attack me,
And through my bowels sorely rack me,
And with cramp-catches, did contract me,
    I roll'd and cried;
Despair and anguish did distract me, –
    I almost died.

Long did I toss, sore vex'd and grieving,
Still physics of all kinds receiving,
My stomach all convuls'd and heaving,
    Repell'd the force;
Some inward barrier, art deceiving,
    Turn'd back its course.

With senna, salts and castor oil,
They drench'd me every little while,
The strong disease such power could foil,
    To yield, full loth,
At length we found the foe recoil,
    At the hot bath.

From thence I date my first relief,
Some small remittance of my grief, –
From thence my puking ceas'd in brief,
    Without delay;
The castor oil led on as chief,
    And found its way.

By appetite, I was deserted,
When colic pains athwart me darted, –
Sleep from my eyes had quite departed,
    I *rose* and *lay*;
Oft from my restless couch I started,
    And wish'd for day.

The night was tedious, long and dreary –
My back, and sides, and limbs, grew weary;
By living fancy, wild and eerie,
    I could espy
A negro's head, red eyes, and bleary,
    Close sitting by.

Emetics, doubtless, rais'd a fume,
The dying taper left a gloom,

Giants and fairies fill'd the room.
  O! mortal Moses!
What awful figures they assume –
  Long teeth and noses!

A female fiend lay cross the bed!
One in the curtain roll'd her head!
A wizard on two chairs lay dead –
  His ghost stood by him;
By glimmering light the fire had made,
  I could descry him!

Then reason took her seat anew,
At sight of her, the spectres flew,
A fairy host, infernal crew,
  All silent whist;
Soon from my bed my limbs I drew,
  Got up and dress'd.

My wife and children, kind did tend me,
With every aid they did befriend me;
With care they strove not to offend me,
  Now peevish grown;
Their very strength they seem'd to lend me,
  When I had none.

My diet was prepared complete,
Thin water gruel, little sweet,
I beans and barley water ate –
  My only food;
Denied of bread, and also meat,
  A fortnight good.

Although I then was faint and feeble,
Thank God, I now can head the table,
And with my knife and fork, am able
  To cut or tear;
And with the rest, can scrape and scrabble,
  To get my share.

But, oh! I soon must leave this port,
My bark unmoor'd again must start;
What seraph guard shall me escort,
    To that bless'd shore?
Where friends of peace and love resort,
    To move no more.

Robert Dinsmoor To Peter Ayer

DEAR SIR – When I was at your house about a year ago, Mrs. Ayer told me that her little girl wished me to write a few verses, and send them to her. The high esteem I then had, and still have, for you and your family, and the pleasure of endeavoring to gratify the little maid, induced me to write the following, which I thought proper to enclose to you. I withheld them till now from an unwillingness to discover my own vanity; but venturing to read them lately to a friend of mine, in whose taste and judgment I have the highest confidence, I was urged to send them. If the lines meet your approbation, I will thank you and your worthy lady to present them to your little daughter, Miss Harriet, as a new year's gift from me. Pardon this freedom in a real friend.

To Miss Harriet Ayer

WHAT poet could refuse to write,
Sweet little Miss, when you invite?
O! might my song your ear delight,
    And sense impart,
And give your mind ideas bright,
    T'improve your heart.

May that young heart, untaught to err,
First learn its Maker to revere,
And wisdom's peaceful paths prefer,
    And vive detest;
And flames of love to virtue fair,
    Glow in your breast.

Your parents' counsels always mind,
And to your tender bosom bind.
Their sober rebukes and cautions kind,
    (From hearts of love,)
Like golden apples you shall find,
    Through life to prove.

And like some beauteous flower in May,
Let all your leaves through life display,
Or, like the rose-bud opening gay,
    Unsullied bloom;
And your sweet innocence convey
    A rich perfume.

May you, among your sisters fair,
Blessings divine and temporal share,
And grace the family of Ayer
    With modest charms;
And soon adorn with beauties rare,
    Some poet's arms.

Should pensive dullness you betray,
Then pore upon his pious lay,
And chant his numbers night and day,
    With lightsome heart;
'Twill drive your anxious cares away,
    And peace impart.

Farewell, my little blushing maid,
To whom this small respect is paid,
May Heaven still guard the paths you tread;
    And make you blest;
'Till down your matron head be laid,
    In peace to rest.

Peter Ayer To Robert Dinsmoor

HAVERHILL, *February* 20, 1813.

DEAR SIR:
I had the honor of receiving your very particular favor of January 8th, together with the beautiful lines to my little daughter. Accept, sir, mine and Mrs. Ayer's warmest thanks for your kind attention; whilst little Harriet is very grateful for her little treasure, she esteems it like "apples of gold in pictures of silver," and does not wonder that her Mamma so much admires the "Rustic Bard." That you may long continue to enrich the world with your poetical numbers, and when you let fall your mantle, it may be caught by some happy Elisha, is the wish of your very much obliged friend, and humble servant.

The Last Of Bonaparte

WHERE'S Bonaparte? – the question now occurs,
Is he in Paris, or the federal city?
Or is he houseless, without boots or spurs,
Disguis'd, unknown, a beggar now for pity?
Has Wellington the bloody tyrant caught?
Does Blucher's arm arrest the fugitive?
Has death itself, with double vengeance fraught,
Cut off his life, who ne'er deserv'd to live?
O, Bellerophon! dost thou him enclose?
Does he to Maitland bow his haughty head,
Yielding submissive to his conquering foes,
And to a British prince for mercy plead?
Does he traverse Northumberland's huge deck,
And far in ocean, with despairing eyes,
Behold St. Helena, as 'twere a speck,
With adamantine walls rais'd to the skies?
While foaming billows round his mansion roll,
And hope is lost in never-ending mist,
Spectres and demons fright his haggard soul!
There Bertrand's wife and he may play at whist.
Saint Helena! thou pre-appointed spot,
That holds the boasted emperor of the world!
There shall his glory, like his carcase, rot,
From pride's high throne by Heaven indignant hurl'd.
So, Lucifer, Omnipotence defied,
And led created armies to rebel!
Though the foul spirit justly might have died,
He gnaws his chains now in the gulf of hell.

WINDHAM, *October*, 1815.

Robert Dinsmoor To Silas Betton

WINDHAM, *February* 1, 1816.

MY DEAR FRIEND:
AGREEABLY to your request, and to fulfill a promise, I made you the last time I saw you, which to me seems a long time, I return you your original letters, with "The last of Bonaparte." You will observe, when it was written, in the month of October last, reports were fluctuating with respect to Bonaparte and his destination. The Haverhill Intelligencer was the principle source of my information, I took things as they were stated, and from week to week, kept writing and doubting, till at length, I found he was fixed on the Island of St. Helena. I doubt whether any merit can justly be attached to the piece, yet I think it may serve as a kind of memorandum to those of my family and friends, who may hereafter read my poems, and show that the fall of that tyrant was not altogether unnoticed by me. I have also enclosed a short address to you, which was written last Thanksgiving Day. You will doubtless recollect you told me you had become a religionist, and that you had in your custody the whole controversy published between the Unitarian and Trinitarian clergy, of Boston, and its vicinity, which you said you were then at your leisure seriously perusing. This, sir, together with my own knowledge of you, from your infancy, and also of the religious sentiments of your worthy, honorably, and pious parents, and likewise of your learned and orthodox preceptor, our late pastor, the Rev. Simon Williams, under the tuition your were fitted for college, will, I trust, sufficiently apologize for my addressing you on that subject, as I have done. One thing I will just mention to you, which I well remember, and dare say you have not forgotten it. When the whole congregation, as was then the custom, had sung the portion of psalms, given out and read by that good old man, he would arise, and present line by line, a Doxology, which I am persuaded was of his own making, for I have never found it just so in any book –

> To Father, Son, and Holy Ghost,
> The God whom we adore,
> Be honor, glory, power and praise,
> Ascrib'd for evermore.

This he did at the close of divine worship for a number of Sabbaths. My uncle Cochran, and I, were then the clerks, and felt obliged to sing; but all the rest of the society, or the principal part of them, sat mute; and before we could get through, the elders, with a number more of our (I was going to say superstitious) old fathers, although I hope, and believe, they are now in heaven would be out of the meeting house, crying Popery! Popery! – He means to bring us all under the Church of England, yet! I intended to have copied your letters before I returned the originals, but Robert goes to school, and my necessary avocations sternly deny me time to do it. This must account for my so criminal delay. A great part of them were stitched into my manuscript book, among some of my own writings, and other friends' letters. I had to cut them out, and may have injured them some; but I think you can make out to read the whole of them. I depend upon having them all again. It is a treasure I wish to leave to my family, and I assure you my book looks as if it had lost half its body, and I am sure it has lost two thirds of its soul. It will be in your power, in due time, to restore what is wanting in both, and even to add to its dignity and lustre. Accept, sir, my sincere love, and give the same to every one of your family, who regard me. When you may have an opportunity, remember me to the Orphan.

P.S. I have withheld all your poetry, and I wish there had been more of it. I have also kept back all that you ever sent me of the Orphan's composition. I will here give you a copy of a few lines which you sent me, accompanying the epitaph written by him.

Thanksgiving Day

When corn is in the garret stored,
And sauce in cellar well secured,
When good fat beef we can afford,
    And things that're dainty,
With good sweet cider on our board,
    And pudding plenty;

When stock, well housed, can chew their cud,
And at my door a pile of wood,
A rousing fire to warm my blood –
    (Bless'd sight to see,)
It puts my rustic muse in mood,
    To sing for thee.

When we of health enjoy a share,
And feast upon some wholesome fare,
Our hearts should rise in grateful prayer.
    And bless the donor
In thankful songs, let voices rare
    Exult his honor.

Perhaps in leisure hours you choose
To pass the time, and to amuse,
The Unitarian scheme peruse;
    But, sir, take heed,
Their subtle reasoning may confuse,
    And wreck your creed.

Lowell and Channing may debate,
As politicians, wise and great,
Predict their country's future fate,
    By reasoning clear;
And shew blind rulers of the State,
    What course to steer;

But shall they teach us to degrade
Him, who is all creation's Head?
The mighty God, who all things made,
    Call him a creature?
Say Godhead never was display'd
    In human nature!

Whoe'er such doctrine well allows,
Debar themselves from Christ's pure house;
Renouncing their baptismal vows,
    As vague and mean;
And infidelity espouse,
    As Deists clean.

Though none can tell how this may be,
That God is one, yet persons three,
Existing from eternity,
    Faith must receive it;
'Tis nought but infidelity,
    To disbelieve it.

Your parents own'd this doctrine true,
And did their solemn vows renew,
E'en when that name was call'd on you,
    With water shed;
Sprinkling like rain or sacred dew,
    Thine infant head.

This doctrine our Great Teacher taught,
To know this mystery, Williams sought,
Though far surpassing human thought,
    He own'd it true;
And deem'd all other sciences nought,
    When this he knew.

As you, dear sir, must witness be,
His pupils sang doxology, –
How oft you've seen his bended knee
    Embrace the ground,
To Three in One, and One in Three,
    In prayer profound!

Like that great man, let you and I,
Believe and practice, 'till we die –
Nor God's electing love deny;
    Then rise and reign
With saints enthron'd about the sky.
    Amen, Amen.

WINDHAM, *December 7*, 1815.

Rev. David M'Gregore To R. Dinsmoor

Did e'er a cuif take up a quill,
Wha ne'er did aught that he did weel,
To gar the muses rant an' reel,
      An' flaunt an' swagger,
Nae doubt ye'll say, 'tis that daft chiel,
      E'en Dite M'Gregore.

To write to Rab, the Rustic Bard,
Is nae sic easy task, but hard,
Syne every line will meet reward,
      Wi' slee inspection,
And shaw itsel' baith blait an' scar'd,
      Wi' imperfection.

When favor'd wi' your kind epistle,
The muse within my breast did nestle,
Though may be I hae bought the whistle –
      A wad-be poet,
My brainless head's sae big'd wi' gristle,
      That ye maun know it.

But Rab's the trustiest o' his kind –
The name gies pleasure to my mind;
His honest heart was ne'er design'd
      To scaith or scare me,
Though every word an' every line
      Will tent to waur me.

Your poem on thanksgiving day,
Cam' safe to han', an' weel I may
Express my sentiment an' say,
      The truth will stan',
Think Unitarians what they may,
      Throughout the lan'.

In days o' yore, the heavenly thrang
O' morning stars in concert sang,
Whan nature a' frae chaos sprang,
    An' time began;
And then the Triune mandate rang –
    "Let *us* make man!"

This sentence does fu' weel agree
To *three* in *ane*, an' *ane* in three;
For angels sure could never be
    Aids in creation –
That wark, we a' may plainly see,
    Ill suits their station.

Th' eternal Son created a',
Uphauds an' rules their earthly ba'
Redeem'd our race frae Adams fa'
    He's surely God.
Socinians ae day maun fa'
    Beneath his rod.

Whan frae the heavens he'll be reveal'd,
In flaming fire his sword to wield,
Then, Unitarian, where's your shield,
    To ward the blow?
Your doom will then nae doubt be seal'd,
    Wi' diels below.

O, could this hamely feckless rhyme
Persuade you to repent in time,
An' turn your thoughts on things sublime
    In Revelation,
Ye aiblins may by grace divine,
    Attain salvation.

Your life wad then be free frae scaith,
An' whan death comes to stap your breath,
Ye'd die triumphant in the faith,
    Though tempest-driven;
An' hopefully resign your breath,
    An' gae to heaven.

But, Rab, the Unitarians try
To gie the word o' God the lie! –
Let us support it manfully,
    Each in our station;
An' prayerfully on Christ rely
    For our salvation.

An' whan death comes, as soon he must,
To gie our bodies to the dust,
Let us commit our soulds in trust,
    To God triune;
Sae, ransomed amang the just,
    We'll win aboon.

BEDFORD, *December* 30, 1816.

Answer To The Rev. David M'Gregore

My rev'rend friend, and kind M'Gregore,
Although thou ne'er was ca'd a bragger,
Thy muse I'm sure naen e'er was glegger –
    Thy Scottish lays
Might gar Socinians fa' or stagger,
    E'en in their days.

Whan Unitarians champions dare thee,
Goliah like, an' think to scare thee,
Dear Davie, fear na', they'll no waur ye;
    But, draw thy sling,
Weel loaded, frae the Gospel quarry,
    Syne gie't a fling.

What though the proud gigantic foe,
Should by fause reasoning strive to show,
An' lay our Saviour's honors low,
    Baith bauld an' fierce, –
Then let the Heaven directed blow,
    His frontlet pierce.

Tent weel, ye're set to guard the truth,
Ye'll fin' fause teachers sly an' smooth,
But clap the trumpet to thy mouth,
    An' gie th' alarm;
The sound, by some, though ca'd uncouth,
    May save frae harm.

If we can trust what Scripture saith,
Christ is our God, an' Saviour baith,
Then let us fix our hope an' faith
    On that foundation;
Wha trusts aught else, maun sink in death,
    An' deep damnation!

Let you an' I, in sweet accord,
To Christ our highest praise afford;
'Tis sure his right to be ador'd,
    As God of all!
Let every creature to the Lord,
    In worship fall!

"RUSTIC BARD."

Robert Dinsmoor To Silas Betton

WINDHAM, *March* 19, 1819.

MY DEAR FRIEND:
THE next morning after returning from Salem, after having spent the evening at your house, I took out your letters, intending to examine every one of them carefully; and in a few moments I found the one so long neglected, of which you so justly upbraided me for not answering. I know not what kind of an excuse to make for myself, for surely it was a criminal neglect. I am persuaded there must have been some very pressing circumstances that caused me to lay that letter out of sight, and forget it. I can make no other satisfaction for my fault, but just beg your forgiveness, and from henceforth write to you till you are tired. Late in the winter of last year, I sent you some letters and poems, and when you returned them, I received the following note from you written on the back of John Nesmith's letter, dated March 27, 1818:

"DEAR SIR:
I acknowledge the receipt of the letters and poems which you sent me, and thank you for them; particularly the pieces written for you two nieces. In transcribing them, I find now new beauties which I cannot here mention. I think, however, the language might be improved without injuring the sentiment or poetry—of this when I see you. You know I never flatter you. I return the letters with my acknowledgements.

SILAS BETTON."

I considered this as the last line I ever received from you, and have often wondered why you did not write and give me your strictures in full.

Your last letter, to which I shall now allude, was written May 20; and it grieves me the more, when I find that you address me as a friend, in your trouble, to whom you always fly whenever any thing ails you.

[In this letter Mr. Betton mentions his riding home from Londonderry one very stormy night, and being without an outward coat, suffered considerably, and took a severe cold. And though he had without medical aid, kept about during the spring, and attended to his farming concerns, he perceived he should get rid of his cold, and the unpleasant cough that attended it, without putting himself under the care of a physician, which he calls fighting the grim monster, death, single-handed; but expresses his determination to do this as soon as the weather becomes milder, and he himself released from the pressure of business. And further makes an offer of some seed corn the Mr. Dinsmoor, this being from the coldness of the former season, an article of difficult procurement. – To this letter the following poem was the Bard's reply.]

Robert Dinsmoor To Silas Betton

DEAR man! and did you suffer so
With cold and rain and driving snow?
O! why did you so careless go,
    Without your cloak,
That sleet might in upon you blow,
    And make you choke?

Why did you not conclude to tarry,
And lodge all night in Londonderry,
Was it that you might be with Mary,
    Your loving wife –
That through much dangers you did worry,
    And risk'd your life?

I'm sure your ride could not be pleasing,
With fingers numb, and almost freezing;
The cold upon your vitals seizing,
    All chilling through –
No doubt your windpipe stuff'd and wheezing,
    Near breathless grew.

In such a plight for you to buckle,
And with the "king of terrors" struggle;
To the "grim beast" you would not truckle,
    Though "single handed!"
Strange that you were not made to knuckle,
    But bravely stand it!

Though you escap'd his fangs but hardly,
I'm pleas'd to think you made him parley,
'Till you could sow your oats and barley,
    And peas and wheat;
And plant your corn, so nice and early,
    For bread to eat.

I think it madness in the man,
Who would lie down if he could stand,
And swallow drugs whene'er he can
 Get time to do it!
"Gae fa' upo' anither plan,"
 Or else you'll rue it.

The generous offer of your corn,
I never wish'd to slight or scorn;
My heart as true as e'er was born,
 Could not refuse it;
As mine was dropp'd that very morn
 I could not use it.

Though times then look'd both dark and drear,
And nought like seed time did appear,
We've liv'd almost another year,
 Nor lack we food;
Then never let us yield to fear –
 The Lord is good.

We live upon his bounteous care,
He rules the seasons of the year;
Nor can we make a single hair,
 Or white or black.
Seed-time and harvest, promis'd fair,
 He'll not take back.

We'll eat and drink, and cheerful take
Our portions, for the Donor's sake;
For thus the Word of Wisdom spake,
 'Man can't do better –
Nor can we, by our labours make,
 The Lord a debtor.'

A sullen saint, if such can be,
Is sure a hideous sight to see;
Hope sets the Christian's conscience free
  From black despair:
With peaceful hearts, let thee and me,
  For death prepare.

John Nesmith To Robert Dinsmoor

October 21, 1817.

DEAR SIR, – I return you your manuscript volume, and with it, my sincere thanks for the pleasure it has afforded me. I have read it over and over again, and every time I have discovered new beauties. When melancholy, I have turned to the "Lament," and always found my attention irresistibly drawn from my own sorrows, to that of the poet's. And lost to every feeling of sympathy, must be the man, who can read of sorrow so finely portrayed without emotion.

I can well excuse Spring's mischief, he laments and confesses so beautifully. Skip moralizes finely. The Farewell to the Muses, is elegantly descriptive. But, why should I, who am no poet, and scarcely competent to write prose, attempt to particularize the peculiar beauties that characterize each of your poems. It may be thought presumption, but I hope not by you. Being called upon to attend customers, I have but just time to subscribe myself your friend.

Robert Dinsmoor To Mary E. Dinsmoor

THE FOLLOWING POEM WAS ADDRESSED TO THE BARD'S NEICE, IN KEENE, ON RECEIVING FROM HER, WHEN VERY YOUNG, A PICTURE OF JOHN BULL, STUNG TO AGONY BY THE WASP AND HORNET, AS A SPECIMEN OF HER DRAWING.

My dear young friend, and kind niece Mary,
My muse has long been dull and weary;
But now, she'd sing and flaunt right airy,
    When fancy sees you:
Yet still, there seems to be a query,
    What theme might please you.

Of politics I shall not sing,
Nor tell how wasps and hornets sting:
My satire darts away I'll fling,
    Like bards before;
Though Bull nor Bona', Duke nor King,
    Shall ever gore me.

Should I assume the jovial strain,
I fear you justly might complain,
And treat my sonnet with disdain,
    Like shy and coyish;
And call your aged uncle vain,
    And light and boyish.

Should I in prose or rhyme descant,
On what perhaps we both most want,
And talk religion like a saint,
    Or "unco guid" –
I might incur a sneering cant,
    Both sharp and shrew'd!

The "rigid righteous" I detest,
Who think their own opinion best,

And fix a standard in their breast,
    Their own production;
And without right or reason, rest
    On false instruction!

But, sure I am, there's something right,
That I'll defend with all my might;
And something wrong, 'gainst which I'll fight,
    With all my power;
And vindicate my cause, in spite
    Of foes that're sour.

Virtue and vice were ne'er design'd,
At once to rule the human mind –
To one or other we're inclin'd,
    Or else oppose;
Nor do we on the thistle find
    The blooming rose.

When by sore sickness we're oppress'd,
No worldly wealth can give us rest;
True virtue seated in the breast,
    Sweet peace can give;
Religion's self can make us blest,
    To die or live.

How lovely does the maid appear,
Whose bosom beats for virtue fair!
She makes religion first her care,
    With spirit meek –
True grace adorns her modest air,
    With blushing cheek.

And should she be a polish'd dame,
High bred, and of scholastic fame,
Her pious heart can ne'er disclaim
    Her heavenly birth;
"A Christian," is the highest name,
    She seeks on earth.

How blest the man whom she shall wed,
And on his bosom lean her head!
No rival lover need he dread,
    But safe confide –
Angels surround their nuptial bed,
    To guard his bride!

And when the fatal hour is come,
That calls her body to the tomb,
She, fearless of her future doom,
    Since hope is given,
Can leave the world without a gloom,
    And fly to heaven!

The joys of sense are transitory,
The scenes of fortune often vary;
May wisdom guide your steps to glory,
    And Heaven approve; –
Sweet peace be yours, my dear niece, Mary,
    And God still love.

Silas Betton To Robert Dinsmoor

SALEM, *March* 29, 1817.

DEAR SIR:
On my return from court, I found the book, with other manuscripts. I have recorded all of them – but have not proceeded any farther. The cold sleety weather makes me unfit for writing. The genial warmth of the Spring, may set me on my legs. I came home from Portsmouth in good health, and have remained so, except an occasional cold or two. I do not think I should have written you at this time, unless to beg a favor, and I will do it in forma pauperis. I want to buy, borrow or beg a half a bushel of good seed corn. I should prefer the latter. The order of nature, totally rendered mine unfit for use. You have enough. Let me have some, remembering when you give to the poor you lend to the Lord. Or, if you are governed by self-interest "cast your bread upon the waters, and you shall receive it in many days."

Robert Dinsmoor To Silas Betton, In Answer To The Foregoing Letter

DEAR SILAS, but I'm wae to hear,
How frost destroy'd your corn las' year,
An' pits ye now in sic a fear,
    About your bread;
Nor can your crowdie caudron steer,
    'Till ye get seed.

Your pleasure sae pithy an' sae pure,
'Tis just the scripture, I am sure;
To liberal sauls, the words secure:
    I'll not deny thee,
Since thou art rank'd among the poor,
    I'll maun supply thee.

I aye was free wi' a' my might,
To help the poor dependant wight.
Nor wad I drive him out at night,
    Amang the snaw;
To warm his bluid, I took delight,
    An' fill his maw.

Although my corn's baith poor and scant,
I'm sure your honor sha'na want;
I canna see thy wame look guant,
    That aye look'd fu';
At your request twa pecks I'll grant,
    The best that grew.

Sure fortune's an unsteady wheel,
That constantly maun row an' reel,
An' gar ane that's sae rich a chiel,
  Begin to dread,
Lest he the pangs o' poortith feel,
  An' lack o' bread.

You wha o' walth might been a bragger,
Doth poortith point at you his dagger?
An' gar your faith an' hope baith stagger,
  Wi' heart sair grievin';
An' turn you fairly out a beggar,
  To seek your livin?

Thy noble saul for honor born,
To stoop sae laigh might think it scorn,
'Twad pierce my heart like any thorn,
  In need to see thee;
Thou ne'er shall want a peck o' corn,
  While I can gie thee.

Soon planting time will come again,
Syne may the heavens gie us rain,
An' shining heat, to bless ilk plain,
  An' fertile hill;
An' gar the loads o' yellow grain,
  Our garrets fill.

Then smiling wives wi' a' their brood,
Shall grace our board in jovial mood,
An' wi' us sup the luscious food,
  Like yankees true,
Syne we will praise the name o' gude,
  Whan we are fu'.

Shame fa' the Queen, that dares despise it,
The King himsel' might highly prize it;
'Tis healsome fare for ane that tries it,
      Wi' Hawkies milk;
She's but a gawkie that denies it,
      Though dress'd in silk.

As lang as I hae food an' claithing,
An' still am hale, an' fier, an' breathing,
Ye's get the corn – an' may be aething,
      Ye'll do for me;
(Though God forbid) – hang me for nothing,
      Without a fee.[1]

A Farewell To Miss M. E. D., Of Keene, The Bard's Neice, After A Visit To Her Friends In Windham

MY dear young friend, I thank you for your visit,
Life's joys are fleeting – happiness what is it?
Farewell my neice – to part is our sure lot,
Soon you'll forget me – and you'll be forgot!
Your uncle, shortly in the dust must sleep;
Then for his sake this small memento keep.
May you ne'er meet with fortune's adverse throws,
Nor frost untimely nip your blooming rose;
May God protect you o'er life's boisterous sea,
And land you safe in blest eternity.

Robert Dinsmoor To Miss Ann Orr, Of Bedford

THIS POEM WAS WRITTEN ON RECEIVING FROM THE YOUNG LADY TO WHOM IT IS ADDRESSED, A SERMON PREACHED BY REV. WALTER HARRIS, OF DUNBARTON, BEFORE THE FEMALE CENT SOCIETY, IN BEDFORD.

DEAR cousin Ann, I got your gift,
Which gave my native pride a lift;
Your father's friend you will not shift,
    Since yours you rank me;
All other cares I'll turn adrift,
    And kindly thank ye.

The truth that springs from wisdom's source,
And runs throughout that grand discourse,
Must strike the infidel with force,
    And deep regret;
And give the atheist keen remorse,
    Perhaps too late!

Let impious souls who never felt,
The piercing pain of sin and guilt,
Lest bowels petrified should melt
    Their hearts, they harden;
Now own a Saviour's blood was spilt,
    To purchase pardon!

To make his glorious gospel spread,
He calls the females to his aid;
The matron saint, and pious maid,
    Their gifts bestow;
That nations who in sins are dead,
    His name may know!

O! may the ladies every where,
Soon emulate the Bedford fair,
And make the cause of Christ their care –
    His light diffuse;
One cent a week each well might spare,
    For such a use.

'Tis not the largest sacrifice,
That's most accepted in his eyes;
The gracious Lord will not despise
    A widow's mite!
A single cent He'll deem a prize,
    If given aright.

By means like these shall Zion rise,
And make her standard to the skies!
Though hell with all its gates annoys,
    Her brazen walls;
The power of darkness, death and lies,
    Like Dagon falls!

Soon gospel light shall spread abroad
To pagans in their dark abode,
And isles where Christians never trod,
    Wait Christ's commands,
And Ethiopia to God
    Stretch out her hands!

Robert Dinsmoor To Henry Davidson

WINDHAM, *April*, 1818.

DEAR SIR:
I have received three letters from you since you left this town last. – The first was written on the 5th of April, the anniversary day that called my dear daughter Jane and your beloved wife, to the world of spirits! Your lines on that occasion were affecting and pathetic. I am well pleased with the motto inscribed on Jane's gravestone. I wrote the following epitaph, as a small memento for her. If you think it worthy, you may give it a place among your manuscripts – and keep it as a remembrancer for her and me. It is thus prefaced:

In memory of Jane Wear Davidson, wife of Mr. Henry Davidson, of Belfast, Me. : and eldest daughter of Dea. Robert Dinsmoor, of Windham, N.H., who died April 5, 1817, in the 34th year of her age. She left her husband and three small children – two sons and a daughter.

> Beneath this stone, here lies alone,
> A loving husband's pride.
> In prime of life, the virtuous wife,
> And tender mother died:
> Her dear remains, this grave retains,
> From father's house afar,
> Beyond our view, her spirit flew,
> Bright twinkling like a star.
> A Christian she – her soul set free,
> Fled from this gloomy shore,
> To worlds of light – and glory bright,
> Where hopes and fears, and pains and tears,
> And death, are known no more!

Although Jane was my own daughter, and notwithstanding all I have written, I think that something more is justly due to her character. I know she was an affectionate and dutiful child, possessing a tender and truly benevolent heart. She was the eldest of 13 children. In the sixteenth year of her age, by the death of her mother, she was left at the head of the ten that survived. The care of my young children, and the affairs of my house she then undertook with the fortitude of an experienced matron; and was really a pattern of economy, frugality and industry. She made a public profession of religion at an early age, and through the whole of her subsequent life, true piety was stamped on her conduct. And in charity, I believe, she was a "Christian indeed." How often does my imagination cause me to view my dear Jane heaving her last gasp – breathing out her soul to God – her eyes closed in death! Stretched out a lifeless corps! Shrouded and placed in a coffin! Then follow her bier to the grave—look into the dismal cell, – where, with a sound of horror, she takes her last abode! Then, turning back, I bid my child farewell!

> Imagination paints the solemn scene –
> I view the bed of expiring Jane;
> With soul serene, faith beaming in her eye,
> I see in her a loving Christian die;
> A mortal paleness fixt upon her cheek,
> With quivering lip, her tongue forbears to speak;
> Her pulses cease! – She gasps in vain for breath,
> And shuts her eyes fast in the sleep of death!
> While dust to dust, she mingles with the dead,
> On seraph wings, to God, her spirit fled!
> To her remains, a just respect is paid;
> I see her shrouded – in a coffin laid;
> Her weeping friends perform each funeral rite;
> The lid and grave cloth, hides her from my sight.
> With pensive step and many a falling tear,
> I in procession follow close her bier;
> At length we reach the sad sequester'd spot,
> Where her dear flesh and bones, are doom'd to rot!
> Her dear remains descend the yawning cell –
> With aching heart, I bid my child farewell!
> Death, lost its sting – the grave no victory won;
> Thanks be to God – she conquer'd through his Son!

Robert Dinsmoor To Sarah Davidson

WINDHAM, *Sept.* 21, 1819.

MY DEAR SALLY: – Let it not surprise you to find this a writing from me. I could not have given it to you with my own hand at home, but I was afraid it might affect you too much. I thought it more my duty to brace you up, and encourage you to persevere in the course you have taken, than to melt your heart with grief, and damp your fortitude with the idea of never seeing me again. Although there is an impression of this kind on my mind, yet I hope I shall be disappointed in my expectation. The enclosed lines are in the form of "A Farewell," set to the tune of "Maj. Andre's Farewell." I do not think them at all elegant, nor to be compared with those of which they seem to be a little in imitation. Nor yet do I think them equal to what I once could have done. You will consider they were written abruptly, and you must therefore make allowances, and accept of them, and keep them as a small remembrancer from me. I was here just about to sign my name; but I must remind you of one thing, which perhaps, you never thought of, and it may seem strange – it is this: you are my fifth daughter, and my sixth child, and you and I have lived more days and years, in one family together, than ever I lived in a family, with father, mother, wife, child, or friend. And you know we have ever been at peace with one another – and I pray, that the God of peace may be with you.

A Farewell

I.

Ah! my dear Sally, must we part,
Grief makes my bosom swell;
O! how can I with aching heart,
Pronounce that word, Farewell?
In silent hours, both night and day,
I'll surely think on thee;
But who can tell, when far away,
If you'll remember me?

II.

Now bound by wedlock's sacred bands,
A mother's care is thine;
If love has join'd your hearts and hands,
My heart shall not repine:
'Tis duty calls you to the place,
Where my Jane used to be;
Perhaps no more to see my face, –
Will you remember me?

III.

That you may live a happy life,
And love connubial find;
Be sure a gentle loving wife,
Will make a husband kind:
When griefs and joys are equal borne,
'Twill comfort give to thee.
O! may you ne'er be made to mourn,
And then remember me!

IV.

Think, Sally, think what I endure,
When I past scenes review;
When your dear mother deck'd my bower,

With numerous gems like you!
These lovely flow'rets, my delight,
Sprung from that blooming tree!
Alas! I've seen that glory blight;
O! then remember me.

V.

And you, my little son, farewell;
May angels be your guard:
God save you from the gates of hell,
And be your great reward:
And when life's ocean you have past,
As o'er a boisterous sea,
May you arrive in heaven at last,
To join in praise with me!

VI.

Farewell, my darling Mary,[2] too,
Your mother's image bright;
May Heaven soon make a saint of you,
To shine in robes of light!
And while grandpa's a pilgrim here,
His prayer shall rise for thee;
"But, who can tell if thou, my dear,
Will e'er remember me?"

VII.

That blessing temporal and divine,
You mutually may share,
With peace, and love, and grace benign,
Shall be my humble prayer;
And when to heaven you lift your eyes,
Upon each bended knee –
Devotion let, as incense rise,
And then remember me.

A Riddle, Which Appeared In Robert B. Thomas's "Farmer's Alamanac", For The Year, 1807

My nature is strange, oft subject to change,
Sometimes with three heads I appear,
With two I converse! but one is perverse;
Nor endued with reason or fear.
Some pretend I've a tail, am female and male,
And to form me both sexes unite.
I am smooth, yet am rough; I'm tender, yet tough;
I'm fair, oft black and oft white.
As to legs I have eight; some small and some great,
But what will surprise you still more,
You plainly may see, that on one side I've three;
On the other side, half half a score.
I'm very devout, I am known all about,
And at church once a week I am found.
All markets I visit, now tell me what is it,
Does in such contradictions abound.

Answer To The Foregoing

To fairly describe, the nation or tribe,
  In which such a monster is found,
I view'd it all o'er, behind and before,
  And fancied I saw it turn round.
A female yet male – three heads and one tail!
  Still changing its nature by turns!
Who knows then, quoth I, but before this thing die,
  Some one of those heads may have horns?
Though tender, 'tis tough; though smooth, it is rough!
  Five legs out of eight on one side!
Of unequal size! at once in surprise,
  I've found out the riddle! I cried.
A sober old couple, which like to ride double,
  To church and to Market their horse;
They talk as they go, that corn is too low,
  Or preaching's too high, that is worse.
Their sulky old nag – his tail he doth wag;
  But the timid old lady still keeps,
Like a modest young bride, both legs on one side,
  While close to her husband she creeps.
Good Almanac maker, perhaps you're a quaker,
  A foe to each bawdy-like fashion;
Should wives ride a straddle, 'twould spoil all your riddle,
  And bring a reproach on the nation.
The riddle propounded, I think I've expounded,
  For the sheets and the raiment I call!
Now, Thomas be handsome, and don't play the Sampson,
  For I've not yok'd your heifer at all.

                              "RUSTIC BARD."

To Dea. S. Whittemore, Salem, Mass

WINDHAM, *March* 13, 1819.

DEAR SIR,

ACCORDING to promise, I enclose to you a few verses addressed to the Presbyterian, or Branch Church in Salem, of which you are a member. The kind treatment I received from you, and your family, at the time of the instalment of the Rev. Mr. Blatchford, and the pleasure I have since had in the company of you, and your good lady, in our late short interview, induced me to send them first to you. When you have perused them, if you think them worthy, it is at your option to communicate them to your friends, particularly to Master Dodge, the Elder. But as he is a learned gentleman, you must beg of him not to be too severe in criticising the lays of the

"RUSTIC BARD."

Address To The Branch Church, In Salem, Mass

THE FOLLOWING POEM WAS WRITTEN AFTER THE INSTALLATION OF REV. MR. BLATCHFORD, AS PASTOR OF THE BRANCH CHURCH, ON WHICH OCCASION, THE BARD ATTENDED, AS A MEMBER OF THE LONDONDERRY PRESBYTERY.

FAIR blooming branch, ordain'd to be
A graft in that illustrious tree,
Whose boughs shall stretch out to the sea,
    O'erhung with fruit;
Where grace, like rivers running free,
    Bedews the root!

Then let this branch forever be,
In beauty like the olive tree;
While all in sweetest harmony,
    And order shine;
Whose roots like Lebanon agree, –
    Her smell like wine.

O! may this branch still flourish fair,
Beneath the great Jehovah's care;
And may a pious Blatchford's prayer,
    For it be heard;
'Till righteousness in clusters rare,
    His work reward!

And may no barren branch be found,
To grieve his heart or cause a wound;
But living fruit on it abound,
    By grace divine;
And peace and love, still flow around,
    Like milk and wine!

Long may this branch in Salem grow,
A type of heavenly peace below;
And God all needful grace bestow,
  And bless you still;
And guard you safe from every foe,
  To Zion's hill.

A Song, By J.N.,
Teacher Of Music In Windham, 1820

I.

THOUGH loud the wint'ry blast does howl,
Far o'er the craggy mountain's brow,
And nature's visage wears a scowl,
Still may our cheerful accents flow.

II.

New-Hampshire's sons, with plenty blest,
May by their social fireside stay,
By no fell tyrant's hand opprest,
'Till winter's storms have howl'd away.

III.

Sweet peace, with lovely aspect smiles,
Around our free and happy land;
Rough winter's hours the song beguiles,
'Till Spring shall come with visage bland.

IV.

Then will the shepherd's grateful lays,
While his rich flocks spread o'er the down,
Resound to our Creator's praise,
And gay delights the season crown!

V.

Cold winter soon will pass away,
The wheels of time swift roll along;
Soon by my native Nashua,
I hope again to wake my song.

VI.

There 'neath the green elm's bough I'll sing,
With nature's choir, my voice I'll raise,
With rapture hail the lovely spring,
And chant our great Creartor's praise.

"MINSTREL OF NASHUA."

Answer To The "Minstrel Of Nashua"

I.

DEAR minstrel of the Nashua,
Thy chording numbers charm my ear;
Thy vocal strains can cheer the day,
And banish winter's stormy fear!

II.

'Though chill the air, and cold's the blast,
That hurls the snowy tempest round,
Songs, peace, and plenty're our repast,
And spring shall with new joys abound.

III.

Welcome sweet minstrel, welcome here,
To teach rusticity thine art;
Thine accents swell the bursting tear!
Thy music thrills through every heart!

IV.

New-Hampshire bards shall catch the song,
And Windham fair shall chant thy lays;
The flowery spring shall come ere long,
Nor foes disturb our happy days.

V.

Sweet harmony with echo's shrill,
From Nashua's rosy banks shall wake!
Resounding back from Jenny's Hill,
Shall sweep o'er Cobbets peaceful lake!

VI.

Then bard and minstrel both shall join,
With nature's choristers, and sing
Anthems of praise, and songs divine,
To nature's God, our Saviour King.

                              "RUSTIC BARD."

January 31, 1820.

Introduction To "Balaam's Answer"

[The following poem was written in answer to a letter from Silas Betton, Esq. Dated May 17, 1819; in which, alluding to a passage of scripture, he says, "O! Balaam! curse ye me this weather." It seems that it had been very rainy for a considerable time, and as a consequence, that some inconvenience had been experienced in the appropriate work of the season. And in his letter, Mr. B. says, that were the course of things under his direction, he would, instead of a long continued rain, have had eight or ten days of warm weather, that the farmers might have got in their seed; and then alternate showers and sunshine, to bring things forward. It is proper, however, to observe, that at the close of the letter, he adds, that "the GREAT I AM knows that I do not call in question His wisdom seriously."]

Balaam's Answer

O BALAK! would you wish to curse,
And make bad weather ten times worse?
Would you invoke a Magii squad,
To counteract the ways of God?
Think ye that all the powers below,
Can make it rain, or shine, or snow?
Or that the infernal sooty host,
Can lay the wind, or stop the frost?
E'en Beor's son as well might try,
With his black art to sink the sky.
Long since you sent for me afar,
To curse your foes in times of war.
Your proffer'd wealth and high promotion,
Cause'd me to try a foolish notion,
When on Mount Pisga's top I stood,
And all the host of Jacob view'd,
In hopes that you would make me rich,
I sought enchantments like a witch!
When I would curse with perverse will,
My tongue was forc'd to bless them still!
Then to Mount Peor's top I flew,
Tried divinations deep and new;
With Moab's rams and bullock's slain,
I strove to bribe the gods in vain!
But witchcraft, sorcery, and spell,
Took no effect 'gainst Israel!
And there I honestly confess'd,
That none can curse what God has bless'd!
Then in a rage you drove me hence,
Without one cent for my expense.
My wicked heart, a slave to greed,
Was sorely mortified indeed!
I mounted on my little beast,
And set my face toward the east,
Chagrin'd and grieved, I cried, alas!

That e'er I smote my honest ass:
For life I fled, and thought it hard
That you would give me no reward;
Though just my fate – my foot was jam'd,
I lost my life and now I'm d—d!
Those who would sinfully be great,
May think upon poor Balaam's fate.
But, now forsooth, to save your pelf,
You'd be a demigod yourself!
Dry[3] Spicket meadows at your pleasure,
And send down showers of rain in measure!
Enough perhaps to suit your plain,
With heat sufficient for your grain.
Omnipotent, if you could be,
Would you regard a wretch like me?
Your favors would be felt by few,
And lacking wisdom as you do,
I'm sure confusion would ensue.
Unlike to God, who's good to all,
Your favors on self alone would fall.

Missionary Hymn – By J.N., "Minstrel"

I.

LET friends of Zion join to sing,
The glory of creation's King;
Let heathen nations catch the sound,
And shout hosannas far around.

II.

Soon may the gospel's glorious light,
Beam far through error's wide-spread night,
May all who own the Christian's name,
The gospel's benefits proclaim.

III.

Ye sons of harmony unite,
Let sacred songs your tongue delight;
O let enchanting music flow,
'Till all our breasts with rapture glow!

IV.

O! could the heathen catch our lays,
Which we at Christian altars raise;
With what glad feelings would they join,
And chant our Saviour's love divine!

V.

May sympathy each bosom move,
Exciting philanthropic love;
May Christian principles obtain,
And bless the world with peaceful reign.

To J.N.

I.

DEAR sir, I deem it sweet employ,
With you to sing, and pray, and praise;
And in God's house it gives me joy,
To hear the Minstrel's sacred lays.

II.

As far as Christian heralds rove,
O'er foreign wilds, and distant plains
There some Newhall, or sacred grove,
Shall ring with thine immortal strains!

III.

Thy hymn, that first in Windham 'rose,
On missionary wings shall soar,
From Hampshire hills, now clad with snows,
To mounts, on Afric's sultry shore!

IV.

There barb'rous tribes of sable hue,
Enwrapt, shall own Immanuel's name;
And temples fill'd with converts new,
A Saviour's honors shall proclaim!

V.

To bless the name of Zion's King,
We'll join in sweet harmonious strains!
Let all the earth in concert sing,
Our God, the great Redeemer reigns!

"RUSTIC BARD."

WINDHAM, *February* 11, 1820.

To Robert Dinsmoor Titcomb
– A Young Namesake

I.

Come to my arms, my smiling boy!
Long may you live, and still enjoy
   The rustic poet's name;
O may you never need to blush,
If call'd the bayonet to push,
   Or turn thy back with shame;
Should usurpation cause alarms,
   Invader's bugle blow,
Then like a patriot, clad in arms,
   Heroic meet the foe;
The field then, ne'er yield then,
   If justice calls you there;
Victorious, and glorious,
   The conqueror's laurels wear.

II.

But never may thy heart rejoice,
At clang of war's detested noise,
   Where wanton foemen meet;
And may you ne'er exult and tell,
How some one in a duel fell,
   Expiring at thy feet.
Th' illicit lover, pass her door –
Be sure with scorn to shun her.
May thy chaste soul those scenes abhor,
Where virtue falls with honor!
   Precisely, and wisely,
     Choose a sweet mate for life;
     Then take her, and make her
   Thy loving friend and wife.

III.

Sweet be her voice, her genius bright,
The muses's friend, and your delight;
   To sooth your aching heart,
Should ever fortune prove unkind,
And growing cares perplex your mind,
   She comfort will impart.
In some fair cottage, form'd to please,
Where rippling waters glide;
And robins sing among the trees,
Long happily reside.
   Let health there, and wealth there,
   Within thy walls abound,
   And neatness, and sweetness,
   Continually be found.

IV.

Now smiling in your parents' arms,
Display your lovely infant charms,
   And move their kind regard.
Anticipation points the day,
When you shall greater powers display –
   The statesman, and the bard,
But higher honor still attain,
Which grace divine insures.
Compar'd to this all else is vain,
A Christian's fame be yours;
   When driving, and striving,
   Through worldly cares, are pass'd,
   Securely, and surely,
   May heaven be yours at last!

WINDHAM, *September*, 1822.

Lines, Written By Joseph Ladd, Merchant Of Belfast, On The Back Of A Dollar Bill, Which He Had Sent To Castine In The Morning, By Way Of Paying A Debt, And It Returned Back To Him In The Evening Of The Same Day, With Twenty More

Leeze me ance mair into my han'
Na lang frae me hae ye been gawin',
But ye maun gang, an' gang ye may –
My meere wants aits, my hawkie hay.
Sae fare ye weel, may ye weel fare,
But come again wi' twenty mair.

In the month of October, 1820, the Bard made a short visit to his friends in Belfast, ME., and when he was just about to leave them, he wrote the following lines in imitation of Burns, and left them with Mr. Ladd, who had treated him with much kindness

>Fare fa' ye Joe, my canty Ladd,
>Nae feckless whim can mak' thee sad;
>Whan gear comes linkin' in ye're glad,
>>An' blithe ye feel;
>Mair frien's like you I wish I had,
>>Wi' hearts as leal!
>Ilk dollar that ye sen' awa',
>May it return ere night wi' twa,
>And peace, an' plenty, bless your ha',
>>An' a' concerns;
>An' nae misfortune e'er befa'
>>Your wife an' bairns.

The above lines were soon afterwards published in the Belfast paper, and copied into several papers in New-Hampshire. – In making the above mentioned visit, the Bard formed a partial acquaintance with the Rev. Mr. F., who shewed him an address to the "Airshire Bard," by a lady in Gorham – and Elizabeth Hamilton's compact with old age.

Mrs. Elizabeth Hamilton's Compact With Old Age

Is that auld age that's tirlin' at the pin?
I trow it is – then haste to let him in;
Ye're kindly welcome frien', na dinna fear
To shaw yoursel', ye'll cause nae trouble here.
I ken there are wha tremble at your name,
As though ye brought wi' ye reproach or shame,
And wha o' thousand lies wad bear the sin,
Rather than own ye for their kith and kin;
But far frae shirking ye as a disgrace,
Thankfu' I am t' have lived to see thy face.
Nor sal I e'er disown ye, nor tak' pride
To think how lang I might your visit bide,
Doing my best to mak' ye weel respected,
I'll no for your sake fear to be neglected;
But now ye're come, an' through a' kinds o' weather,
We're doom'd frae this time forth to joy thegether;
I'd fain make compact wi' ye firm and strang,
On terms o' fair gif gaff to hand out lang;
Gin thoul't be civil, I sal liberal be –
Witness the lang, lang list o' what I'll gie.
First then, I here mak' ow'r for gude an' aye,
A' youthfu' fancies, whither bright or gay;
Beauties an' graces, too, I wad resign them;
But sair I fear twad cost ye fash to find them;
For 'gainst your daddy, time, they could na stand,
To bear the grip o' his unsonsy hand!
But there's my skin, whilk ye may further crunkle,
An' write your name at length in ilka wrunkle.
On my brown locks ye've leave to lay your paw,
An' bleach them to your fancy white as snaw.
But look na' age, sae wistfu' at my mouth,
As gin ye lang'd to pu' out ilka tooth!
Let them, I do beseech, still keep their places,
Though gin ye wish't, ye're free to paint their faces:

My limbs I yield ye, and if ye see meet,
To clap your icy shackles on my feet,
I'se no refuse; but if ye drive out gout,
Will bless ye for't, an' offer thanks devout.
Sae muckle wad I gie wi' right guid will;
But oh! I fear that mair ye look for still,
Then by that fell glower an' meaning shrug,
Ye'd slap your skinny fingers on my lug;
An' unco fain ye are I trow an' keen,
To cast your misty powders in my een:
But O! in mercy spare my poor wee twinkers,
An' I for ay will wear your chrystal blinkers!
Then 'bout my lugs I'd fain a bargain mak'.
An gie my han' that I sal ne'er draw back.
Weel then – wad ye consent their use to share,
Twad serve us baith an' be a bargain rare.
Thus I wad hae't; whan babbling fools intrude,
Gabbling their noisy nonsense lang an' loud:
Or whan ill nature weel brush'd up wi' wit,
Wi' sneer sarcastic tak's its aim to hit;
Or whan detraction, meanest slave o' pride,
Spies out wee fau'ts, an' seeks great worth to hide:
Then mak' me death, as deaf as deaf can be,
At a' sic times my lugs I lend to thee.
But when in social hour ye see combin'd,
Genius and wisdom – fruits o' heart an' mind,
Good sense, good humor, wit in playfu' mood,
An' candor, e'en frae ill extracting good;
Oh, then auld frien', I maun hae back my hearing,
To want it then wad be an ill past bearing.
Better to lanely sit i' the dowf spence,
Than catch the sough o' words without the sense;
Ye winna promise? Och, ye're unco dour,
Sae ill to manage and sae cauld an' sour.
Nae matter – hail an' sound I'll keep my heart,
Nor frae a crum o't sal I ever part;
Its kindly warmth sal ne'er be chilled by a'
The cauldest breath your frozen lips can blaw.

Ye need na fash your thum, auld carl, nor fret,
For there affection shall preserve its seat.
An' though to tak' my hearing ye rejoice,
Yet spite o' you I'll still hear friendship's voice.
Then though ye tak' the rest it shanna grieve me,
For ae blithe spunk o' spirits ye maun leave me,
An' let me tell you in your lug, old age,
I'm bound to travel wi' ye but ae stage.
Be't lang or short, ye canna keep me back,
An' when we reach the end o't ye maun pack;
For there we part forever, late or air,
An' ither guess companion meets me there;
To whom ye, nill ye will ye, maun me bring,
Nor that I'se be wae, or laith to spring,
Frae your poor dozen'd side, ye carl uncouth,
To the bless'd arms of everlasting youth,
By him, whate'er ye've rifled, stown, or ta'en,
Will a' be gi'en wi' interest back again;
Frost by a' gifts a' graces, thousands moe
Than heart can think o', freely he'll bestow.
Ye need na wonder then, nor swell wi' pride,
Because I kindly welcome you, as guide
To ane sae far your better. Now a's tauld,
Let us set out upo' our journey cauld;
Wi' nae vain beasts, nor vain regrets tormented,
We'll e'en jog on the gate, quiet and contented.

Address To Mrs. S. G., of Londonderry, Accompanying The Foregoing Poem

MY much respected, venerable dame,
Friend of my youth, in age the same I claim,
The Bard's kind patron, lover of the muse,
Who e'en my rustic lay, with candor views;
But oh, dear madam, far superior lays
I here enclose you, worthy of your praise.
Good sense, in simple elegance well dress'd,
By Scottish genius suited to your taste.
Poetic beauties sweetly grace the page,
To sooth the heart, and smooth the brow of age;
With placid face, peace and contentment smile,
And innocence decripitude beguile.
See virgin beauties blooming in their prime,
Calmly surrender'd to the grip of time.
Her charms she yields, and counts it no disgrace
To let old age print wrinkles on her face;
Her locks to whiten, freely gives him leave,
And when her feet are shackl'd, does not grieve!
About her lugs she makes a bargain rare,
Nor will she quite her poor twinkers spare;
No more to hear, would be surpassing grief,
Although at times he's free to make her deaf.
Auld age she flatters, treats him as a friend,
Jogs by his side until their journey's end;
Her uncouth guide gives her no anxious care,
In hopes to meet a better partner there.
When irksome sloughs, and ups, and downs, are past,
Of graces stript, she jilts him at the last;
Immortal youth receives her in his arms,
Arrayed in glorious, uncreated charms!
Vigor restored, she walks the flowery plains,
With soul enwrapt with new extatic strains.
In paradise, she scents the blissful grove,
Where trees of life yield lasting fruits of love,

In light refulgent, basks in heavenly rays,
Where pleasures roll as endless as her days!
But, let no bard presume those joys to paint,
Which are reserved in heaven for every saint.
Lord make them thine, shall be my fervent prayer,
And let e'en me be bless'd, and meet you there.
"Hope humbly then, with trembling pinions soar,
Wait the great teacher death, and God adore."

"RUSTIC BARD."

WINDHAM, *Feb.* 14, 1824.

Verses Addressed To Robert Burns
The Airshire Poet[4]

Fare fa' ye Robie, canty callan,
Wha rhym'd as maist as weel as Allen,
An' pleasant highlan' lads an' lawlan',
    Wi' your auld gab;
May never wae come near your dwallin',
    Nor scaith nor scab.

I've read your warks wi' muckle glee,
Auld lucky nature, there I see,
Has gi'en ye genius like a bee,
    To suck the flowers;
Whare'er ye gang, weel met ye be –
    Blithe be your hours.

Let college sumphs glib Horace praise,
Gie auld blin' Homer still the bays,
An' about Virgil mak' a phrase;
    A guid Scotch taste,
Prefers your ain untutor'd lays,
    To a' their best.

Let them like gauks auld Latin speak,
An' blether out their brak'-jaw Greek,
Though ye were born whar' hills are bleak,
    And cauld winds blaw;
An' though frae buiks nae helps ye seek,
    Ye ding then a'!

May independence be your lot,
To gar the musie frisk an' trot;
An' may ye never want a groat,
    To drown your care,
Whan ye put on your Sunday's coat,
    To rant or fair.

Whan lavrocks tune their bonny throats,
An' i' th' lift, pour forth their notes:
When bleating yeaws first lea' their cots,
    An' clim' the braes,
While roun' the dam ilk lamie trots,
    An' frisks an' plays;

O, Rob! 'tis pleasant then to stray
Whar' little burnies steal away,
And hazeles shield frae Phoebus' ray,
    An' muse an' think,
An' while the breezes roun' ane play,
    Mak' verses clink.

Aft man – but oh! these days are gane,
Have I those doited a' alane,
Or sat upon a foggy stane,
    Beneath a brae,
Whar' Philomel has made her mane,
    And sang her wae.

From rural scenes I've lang been torn,
An' mony a skelp frae fortune borne,
Lamentin' that o' life's gay morn,
    I'm now bereft;
I see nae rose, but fin' the thorn
    Alane is left.

O, man! whan years hang o'er the back,
An' bend us like a muckle pack,
Life then will scarce be worth a plack;
    For mirth and glee,
To younger swankies in a crack,
    Frae us maun flee.

Auld time, that jinkin' slip'ry chiel,
Ere lang will mak' us end our reel,
An' a' our fire an' spirits queel,
    An' quench the low,
That now within our breast's we feel,
    And bleach our pow.

Let us the present haur then sieze,
And reckon gain what the neist gies,
It's vain for what nane o' us sees,
    Our heads to fash,
Or yet permit the warld to teeze
    Us wi' its trash.

Could I, O Rab, but brak' my tether,
An' ony whar' wi' you forgether,
I'm sure we'd souple baith our leather,
    I'd lay my lugs,
We'd mak' our hearts as light's a feather,
    Wi' reaming jugs.

The Bard's Answer To Mr. F. Was Published In Belfast, In The Following Manner: – "For The Hancock Gazette. Lines Written By A Gentleman To A Friend In This Town, After Receiving From Him A Copy Of The "Address To Robert Burns," Which Was Printed In The Belfast Gazette, Some Time Since; With A Request That He Would Send Him "Mrs. Hamilton's Compact With Old Age," Which Appeared In One Of The Christian Disciples, For The Last Year"

My late ken'd frien' o' reverend fame,
Saf' to my hand these verses came,
Compos'd by some auld farran dame,
    The wale o' muses;
The Airshire poet's deathless fame,
    Sweetly she rooses.

Fair poetess, whar' does she dwell?
On moorland, mount, or flowery dell?
Whas sweet harmonious numbers swell,
    To Burns's honour!
If ken'd by me, I'd ware mysel',
    Some notes upon her.

Our restlin' bards their gabs may steek,
She waurs them a' as clean's a leek,
An' wi' her native genius sleek,
    Parnassus speels;
And lea's auld Latin bards an' Greek,
    A' at her heels.

I doubt na she's a Gorham lady,
Sprang frae a Caledonian daddy,
Wha in auld Scotia's tongue sae ready,
    Attunes sic lays,
An' taks frae bards in highland plaidy,
    Their laurel bays.

Were she some Aborigine squaw,
That sings sae sweet by nature's law,
I'd meet her in a hazle shaw,
    Or some green loany,
An' mak' her tawny phiz an' a'
    My welcome crony.

But aiblins she's some bonnie dear,
Whas wit an' beauty few can peer,
Though words that masculine appear,
    Might gar ane rue;
Shamefa' her jugs, for maist I fear,
    She'll whiles get fou'!

The bonnie present ye hae made me,
Has under obligation laid me:
Oh! wad the muses deign to aid me,
    To sing an' rhyme;
Soon should a recompense be paid ye,
    In chords sublime.

But gif ye like to please your frien',
Though our acquaintance short has been,
Ye'll sen' me neist the bargain 'tween
    Auld age, an' youth;
Whar' Lucky barter'd off her een,
    An' her last tooth.

Monody On The Death Of Silas Betton, Esq., To Lieut. Pearson Titcomb of Salem, N.H.

WHAT sad and solemn news do we hear, Pearson T.,
That strikes to our hearts with a knell?
Our friend Betton is gone, and lies cold as a stone,
And weeping, our sorrows we'll tell.
      A-well, a-well-a-day!
And weeping, our sorrows we'll tell.

No more shall we meet this dear friend, Pearson T.,
No more will he urge us to sing,
These sweet Scottish airs, to banish our cares,
Nor his voice in the concert shall ring.
      A-well, a-well-a-day!
Nor his voice in the concert shall ring.

The Gazette itself seem but dull, Pearson T.,
Where we often found genius and glee;
For, low with the dead, they have laid his sage head,
And no poet is sanction'd by Z.[5]
      A-well, a-well-a-day!
And no poet is sanction'd by Z.

Our country in weeds, may lament Pearson T.
And the widow and orphan shall mourn!
He in councils of state, held a place with the great.
And the patriot shall weep o'er his urn.
      A-well, a-well-a-day!
And the patriot shall weep o'er his urn.

Ah! farewell to our patron and friend, Pearson T.,
And in peace let his ashes still rest.
Then while life remains, or blood flows in our veins,
His memory shall live in each breast.
   A-well, a-well-a-day!
His memory shall live in each breast.

February 2, 1822.

Pearson Titcomb To Robert Dinsmoor

THE heart rending news is too true, Robert D.,
Our friend, our lov'd Betton lies low;
Fast clos'd are his eyes, and the sobs and the sighs,
Of his friends, speak their anguish and wo.
      A-well, a-well-a-day!
Of his friends, speak their anguish and wo.

We ne'er shall again hear his voice, Robert D.,
No more shall his silence be broke;
For mute is that tongue, where oft we have hung
With delight, on each theme when he spoke.
      A-well, a-well-a-day!
With delight, on each theme when he spoke.

Cold, cold is that heart which late thobb'd, Robert D.,
The poor their lost friend will deplore;
With the means he was blest, to relieve the distrest,
But their patron and friend is no more.
      A-well, a-well-a-day!
But their patron and friend is no more.

I follow'd his corpse to the grave, Robert D.,
I saw it lower'd into the ground;
The cold turf they press'd, on his motionless breast;
And mournful to me was the sound.
      A-well, a-well-a-day!
And mournful to me was the sound.

Farewell to our late mutual friend, Robert D.,
His exit a lesson imparts;
But while on this earth, a just sense of his worth
Shall be cherish'd in each of our hearts.
      A-well, a-well-a-day!
Shall be cherish'd in each of our hearts.

February 3, 1822

Robert Dinsmoor To A Friend, When The Writer Was Confinded With The Palsy, And Hearing Of Number Of Deaths Among His Friends

HOW awful and solemn the sound,
Of death that still reigns in my ear!
My uncle lies cold in the ground,
With many kind friends I lov'd dear!
How happy the hours we have past,
In circles, to meet now no more!
Those sweet scenes are gone with a blast,
And left me those scenes to deplore!
The world, how delusive its charms!
When all seems delightful and fair,
We're oft seized with sudden alarms,
And taken like birds in a snare!
How quickly our years pass away,
They fly like the cold stormy blast!
The year that commences to day,
To-morrow may prove it our last.
We reason and sense may retain,
When vigor and action are fled;
And feel neither sickness nor pain,
Yet find half our members are dead![6]
In stupor that hand and foot lies,
Which once gave me pleasure to use;
T' accomplish my fond enterprise,
They aid and assistance refuse.
In vain we seek happiness here,
Where troubles incessant abound;
Our joys often end with a tear,
And pleasure itself gives a wound!
In humble submission I'll lie,
And all my vain prospects give o'er;
On Heaven for comfort rely,
And trust in my weak limbs no more.
Farewell to the world and its joys,

I'll court its false favors no more;
My soul up to God shall arise,
And a Saviour's free mercy adore.
Sweet peace there forever shall grow,
And there shall the weary find rest;
There rivers of pleasure still flow,
To drown all the cares of my breast.

January 1, 1823.

The Bard Having Observed In The Gazette And Patriot, Printed In Haverhill, Of Which He Was A Patron, The Following Paragraph, It Is Here Inserted As An Apology For The Answer

"PAY ALL MEN."

The post-riders and proprietor respectfully inform the patrons of the Gazette and Patriot, that they are compelled to request speedy attention to the above text, professing a deep and solemn conviction of the religious and moral duty it enjoins, and feeling the necessity of impressing the minds of delinquent subscribers with the high importance of obeying the precepts of the apostles, and particularly the one above written by him of Tarsus. At the present crisis of affairs, they cannot but indulge the hope, that the foregoing text will command the serious attention of all good citizens. Possessing a great and lively interest in the temporal welfare of their patrons, they cannot refrain from urging them to "pay all men," and thereby exhibit their religious observance of the principle which is inculcated, and their cheerful practice of the punctuality which is enjoined in this salutary admonition. But they deem it unnecessary to expatiate at "learned length" in words of "thundering sound" on the duty obligatory to all men, to "pay all men," as it is a truth so palpable that it needs no illustration; therefore they announce that the bills for subscription, as well as for advertising, will be ready for settlement by the 31st inst.

Haverhill, Dec. 13.

Answer To The Call In The Gazette And Patriot

DEAR Reinhart, Haverhill printer, spare me,
Your text and your doctrine almost scare me,
Delinquents all without restriction,
Must blush, like one, with deep conviction;
You are no drone, or common teacher,
But just a modern, pungent preacher,
Not mangling texts, or wresting scripture,
To cause disputes, and raise a rupture;
No long comment to drown the sense,
With vain parade of eloquence.
The text alone set at the head,
Is proof enough for all that's said;
I wish that teachers not a few,
Would leave their texts unhurt like you.
Preachers there are, who sometimes draw,
Wrong inferences from the law;
'Bout points and tenets, fight like cocks,
But I'll pronounce you orthodox.
Though humbling to my carnal pride,
Both law and gospel's on your side!
Far in arrears, I frankly say it,
But think not sir, I'll never pay it;
Take not thy servant by the throat,
Nor strip me of my thread-bare coat;
That would be usage hard indeed,
But mercy's all that I can plead!
See at your feet my Bardship fall,
"Have patience, and I'll pay thee all."

"RUSTIC BARD."

The Author To His Friend Col. Silas Dinsmoor,[7] Of Mobile, Alabama. In Scotch, The Dialect Of Their Ancestors

DEAR cousin, could I ance mair see thee,
My house should kindly welcome gie thee;
Nae warldly care should gar me lea' thee,
    Nor dumpish be;
Ae week at least I'd spend it wi' thee,
    In cracks an' glee.

Though time all nature doth efface,
Wi' you I'd view our native place,
Whar' sprang a numerous Dinsmoor race,
    Roun' Jenny's Hill;
An' down its brow some burnie trace,
    Or wimpling rill.

Our great grandsire fam'd and rever'd,
In Londonderry lies interr'd!
There, at his head wi' kind regard,
    We'd pile some stanes,
Renew the turf, and right the swaird,
    That co'ers his banes![8]

Whan we our ancient line retrace,
He was the first o' a' our race,
Cauld Erin ca' his native place,
    O' name Dinsmore!
And first that saw wi' joyfu' face,
    Columbia's shore!

Though death our ancestors has cleeket,
An' under clods them closely steeket;
Their native tongue we yet wad speak it,
    Wi' accent glib;

And mark the place their chimney's reeket,
      Like brithers sib.

The progeny that frae them sprang,
O may they a' remember lang,
Their pious prayers, an' haly sang
      O' sacred lays!
Baith e'en an' morn, their dwellings rang,
      Wi' notes o' praise!

In deep devotional reflection,
While memory lasts, sweet recollection
Shall mind their prayers for our protection,
      Wi' hearts sincere;
Syne o'er their dust, wi' kind affection,
      We'd drap a tear!

To cousin Rabin, as ye ca' me,
Ye'd out the city Mobile draw me,
An' Indian tales 'bout Alabama,
      Shrewdly ye'd tell 'im;
An' a' Louisiana shaw me,
      Imprest on vellum.

Their mountains, glens, and forests drear,
Wi' lakes immense, an' rivers clear,
Deep pits, an' dens, enough to fear,
      A savage sable!
On parchment stampt a' wad appear,
      As smooth's the table!

The bard then forth his warks wad bring,
Some tender strain he'd gar thee sing,
Or, read the fau'ts o' poor wee Spring,
      An's frank confession!
Or else some ither funny thing,
      In his possession!

Freely his book he'd lend to you,
(A favor he confers on few.)
An' let you read his poems through,
    An extra volume;
An' mak' remarks in strict review,
    On ilka column.

Nae doubt ye'd candidly inspect it,
An' gently wi' your han' correct it;
Yet if some part should be rejected,
    I'd no' think hard;
But for your pains ye'd be respected,
    B' the "Rustic Bard."

But to few days my life is stinted,
Therefore I modestly would hint it;
I ken my writings will be printed,
    No distant date;
If I were gane, nane could prevent it;
    I dread their fate!

O! could some frien' concert a plan,
To save the credit o' the man,
Whas character maun sink or stan'
    Wi' his production!
Will ye na save me if ye can,
    Frae dire destruction?

Though ye may hae, as I doubt not,
Afar frae hence, a happy lot;
But, can your frien's be a' forgot,
    'Bout Jenny's Hill?
Sweet recollection o' that spot,
    Maun please you still.

Dear Silas, I your frien'ship claim,
Wha bears your honor'd grandsire's name,
Sprung frae that stock, our bluid the same,
    Baith Dinsmoors true!
Fain would I trust my Bardship's fame,
    In care o' you.

Antiquity – The Auld Gun

To pope, or prelate, or pretender,
Nae Dinsmoor arms would e'er surrender;
True protestants, a noble gender,
    Ca'd Presbyterian!
For them, I was a bauld defender,
    Says th' antiquarian.

Whan master brought me to this land,
I aye stood charged at his right hand;
Nae Indian warrior e'er could stand,
    Against Dinsmore![9]
My hail was death, at his command,
    Wi' thundering roar!

Me as his ain, I aye could claim
At "number four," he rais'd my fame,
Wi's Jocteleg – when far frae hame,
    He rudely cut
Th' initials o' his honor'd name
    Upon my butt!

The Following Letter, Is An Answer To I. A. D., The Bard's Nephew, Who Had Written To Him With A View To Rectify Some Misunderstanding Between Them

DEAR nephew, I received your letter –
Scarce aught could please your uncle better,
Displaying genius, sense and matter,
    With friendship fraught;
That I should thus become your debtor,
    I never thought.

Something I own, from me is due,
For proffer'd friendship pure and true;
I never lost my love for you,
    By harsh reflections;
Then cheerfully we will renew
    Those kind affections.

Though passion sometimes bears the sway,
And carries reason quite astray,
I'm never kept a single day,
    In its control;
But deep remorse, and conscience prey,
    Upon my soul!

Anger was never known to rest,
But in the simple foolish breast;
Of that, I hope your not possess'd,
    Nor yet inherit
Malicious feelings, but detest
    That hateful spirit.

Of that base fiend call'd enmity,
I think my heart was ever free;

Let not that foe permitted be,
    To reign, or rule us,
And break the peace of you and me,
    And shame and fool us.

Doubtless you are my kinsman near,
The evidence is strong and clear;
Those kindling sparks that now appear,
    May cause a flame,
To melt the heart, or dry the tear,
    And raise your fame.

A talent I discern in you,
Which by your verse* is brought to view –
'Tis nature's gift bestow'd on few,
    Be sure to use it;
And let the muse with prudence shew
    You don't abuse it.

Since to be useful you incline,
Endeavor nature to refine;
Then, like a gem upon the vine,
    Expand and grow;
And laurel wreaths may yet entwine,
    A Dinsmoor's brow.

                      "RUSTIC BARD."

---

* *The verse alluded to is the following :*

"DEAR RUSTIC BARD:
Teach me thy poetic art,
T' inspire the fancy of the heart,
To scatter words in verse sublime,
As thou didst in thy early prime."

Robert Dinsmoor To John Orr, Esq. Of Bedford, On Returning Young's Night Thoughts, March 1786

WHEN northern winds tempestuous blow,
And hurl around the flakes of snow,
I, shelter'd in my little tent,
Perusing what your kindness lent,
No furious blast disturbs my peace,
While thoughts sublime my heart solace.
Like the poor slave who strives all day,
His cruel master to obey;
Who, if releas'd for half an hour,
And that short time be in his power,
Would to the pool, or plain, resort,
And innocently play and sport,
Enjoying freedom for a while,
Forget his arduous task and toil;
So flies my heart from carking care,
Which binds the sordid in despair;
And by this pleasing pastime find,
It recreates my weary mind.
To trace the poet in his flight,
From the dark shades of gloomy night,
Exploring nature in her rise,
From nought, to worlds above the skies,
All starting forth in strict gradation,
The wond'rous works of God's creation,
Where ends the sight of my dim eye,
I vainly think that there's the sky;
Had I a glass to help my sight,
To view the heavenly curtain right,
E'en that would all abortive prove,
Since it would in proportion move.
So proves the poet's aid to me,
Though curiously he makes me see
Those prospects new, and lengthen'd sight,

Sets larger bounds to infinite!
Aloft upon his wing I'm tost,
And in immensity am lost!
I dream awhile, and pensive pause,
At last I'm found just where I was!

An Ode, Written At The Request Of the Committee Of Arrangements For The Celebration Of Independence, Windham, July 4, 1825

Now let our cheerful voices rise
To God, who built the earth and skies;
And in his temple loud proclaim,
The honors of his sovereign name.

While we our grateful homage pay,
Let freedom's banners wide display;
And hail the bright auspicious morn,
That saw our happy nation born!

Look back, ye honor'd veterans few,
Whose locks are thin, of silver hue,
That ran at war's loud piercing thrill,
To Lexington and Bunker's Hill!

When Charlestown's flame in pillars rose,
Caus'd by our cruel British foes;
Midst thundering cannon, blood and fire,
You saw Lord Perry's host expire!

With fault'ring tongue you yet can tell,
Where some dear friend, or brother, fell;
With palsied limbs, and glimm'ring eyes,
Point to the place where Warren lies!

How chang'd the scene! now horror's past,
With joy behold the great contrast:
No British flag, or rampart there,
But columns rise to freedom fair!

Look back to Bennington, and see
A Stark make Burgoyne's army flee!
Behold that army captur'd quite,
By Gates, on[10] Saratoga's height!

'Twas not our arm the victory gain'd—
The Lord's right hand our cause maintain'd;
For us, th' oppressor's arm He brake,
And saved us for his own name sake!

Columbia now in sweet accord,
Sing loud hosannas to the Lord;
Who makes our eyes with transport see,
This happy day, our Jubilee!

A Scrap – Robert Dinsmoor To Dea. Issac Cochran, Of Antrim, N.H., His Mother's Brother, Who Was A Lieut, At The Taking Of Gen. Burgoyne, Oct. 17, 1777. A Short Review Of That Expedition[11]

My faithful friend, and uncle, kind,
I would bring some things to your mind,
Which still impress'd on mine I find,
    By recollection;
That seems my heart with yours in bind,
    In strong affection.

From my first dawn of life you've known me;
When nature on the world had thrown me,
You did a first-born nephew own me,
    Or younger brother;
And friendship ever since have shown me,
    Kind like my mother.

Childhood and youth, manhood and age,
You've been my friend in every stage;
Sometimes in sport, we would engage
    Our nerves to try;
Sometimes, t'explore the music page,
    The genius ply.

When British laws would us enthral,
Our country for defence did call;
Then martial fire inspir'd us all,
    To arms we flew;
And as a soldier, stand or fall,
    I went with you!

O'er western hills we travell'd far,
Pass'd Saratoga the site of war,
Where Burgoyne roll'd his feudal car,
    Down Hudson's strand;

And Gates, our glorious western star,
    Held high command.

From the green ridge, we glanc'd our eyes,
Where village flames illum'd the skies,
Destruction there was no surprise,
    On Hudson's shore!
Though smoke in burning pillars rise,
    And cannons roar!

But to fort Edward[12] we were sent,
Through icy Bartenskiln we went,
And on that plain we pitch'd our tent,
    'Gainst rain and snow;
Our orders there, was to prevent
    The flying foe.

By counter orders, back we came,
And cross'd the Hudson's rapid stream,
At Schuyler's Mills,[13] of no small fame,
    Thence took our post,
Near Burgoyne's line, with fixed aim,
    To take his host!

With courage bold, we took the field,
Our foes no more their swords could wield,
God was our strength, and He our shield,
    A present aid!
Proud Burgoyne's army there did yield,
    All captive made!

Great Britain's honor there was stain'd.
We sang a glorious victory gain'd!
From hence our States a rank obtain'd,
    'Mongst nation as great;
Our future glory was ordain'd,
    As sure as fate!

To Windham, back with joy we turn'd,
Where parents dear our absence mourn'd;
And our fair friends in rapture burn'd,
    To see our faces!
Sweet pearly drops their cheeks adorn'd,
    In our embraces!

When all our vanquish'd foes were fled,
Love, peace, and harmony were shed,
Like oil descending on the head,
    Or milk or wine;
Williams,[14] the man of God us fed,
    With food divine.

O! let not you and I forget,
How often we've together met,
Like Heman, and Jeduthon,[15] set
    In God's own house;
And solemnly his table at,
    Renew'd our vows!

And when the sacred scene was past,
We sang Doxology at last,
To Father, Son, and Holy Ghost,
    United Three!
One God, our souls redeemed hast,
    So let it be!

While reason in her seat remains,
And blood runs streaming through my veins,
Or memory her power retains,
    I shall review,
And think upon the various scenes,
    I've pass'd with you.

WINDHAM, *May* 12, 1820.

Ode, Sung At The Dedication Of The New Brick School-House, In Windham

I.

COME let our social voices raise
A hymn, to our Creator's praise,
Who makes us see with joyful eyes,
This beauteous dome from ruin[16] rise.

II.

O, may almighty power and grace,
Watch o'er, and guard this sacred place,
Long may these walls repel the storm,
Shelter our youth, and keep them warm.

III.

Let not this building stand in vain,
Like Babel's tower, on Shinar's plain,
Nor let a pedant's drawling sound,
E'er enter, language to confound.

IV.

May this a seat of science be,
And knowledge spring from error free;
May pious precepts here be taught,
And form the bent of every thought.

V.

May virtuous teachers here preside,
Who wisely shall their pupils guide,
And hither let our children meet,
Like students, round Gamaliel's feet.

VI.

Here let young minds like flowers expand,
And spread sweet science o'er the land;
Hence, matrons, rise, and sages great,
To ornament both church and state.

VII.

Here let the tree of knowledge grow,
And streams of love and virtue flow;
Let nothing ever cast a stain,
While time and nature last – amen.

The Braes Of Glenniffer, By Tannahill: Presented By Miss Elizabeth Williams, To the "Rustic Bard"

FOR the following tender and pathetic stanzas, says the Baltimore Patriot, we are indebted to the name of Tannshill,[17] a name that will long be dear to the lovers of Scottish song. His private life is involved in obscurity. He respired the ethereal flame, while he plied the shuttle in a weaver's shop, in Glasgow, and displayed in his effusions that exquisiteness of sensibility which little accorded with his humble lot. The same morbid feelings that produced the phrenzy of Collins, the melancholy of Cowper, the wildness of Chatterton, the intemperance of Burns and Dermody, is exhibited in the untimely fate of Tannshill, whose body was found in the Clyde.

The Braes Of Glenniffer

KEEN blaws the wind o'er the braes o' Glenniffer,
The auld bastle turrets are cover'd wi' snaw!
How chang'd sin' the time that I met wi' my lover,
Amang the green bushes by Stanley green shaw!

The wild flowers o' simmer were springing sae bonny,
The mavis sang sweet frae the green birken tree!
But far to the camp they hae march'd my dear Jonnie,
An' now it is winter wi' nature an' me.

Then ilk thing around us was blithesome an' cheerie,
Then ilk thing around us was bonnie an' braw;
Now naething is heard but the wind whistling dreary,
Now naething is seen but the wide spreading snaw.

The trees are a' bare, and the bird mute an' dowie,
They shake the cauld drift frae their wings as they flee;
They chirp out their plaints seeming wae for my Jonnie,
'Tis winter wi' them, an' its winter wi' me.

You cauld sleety cloud as it skiffs the bleak mountain,
An' shakes the dark firs on its stey rocky brae,
While down the deep glen bawls the snaw-flooded fountain,
That murmur'd sae sweet to my laddie an' me.

'Tis na the loud roar o' the wint'ry wind swallowin',
'Tis na the cauld blast brings the tear i' my e'e;
For o gin I saw but my bonnie Scot's callan,
The dark days o' winter were simmer to me!

Robert Dinsmoor To Miss E. Williams, With A Copy Of "Mrs. E. Hamilton's Ain Fireside"

DEAR Betsey, I've copied "The Braes o' Glenniffer,"
Those beautiful stanzas, o' Tannshill wi' pride,
O! wae worth the fortune, that left him to suffer,
His glory and fame to be drown'd in the Clyde!

How faithfu' to nature he paints the fair maiden,
Caress'd by her lover at "Stanley green shaw!"
But mute are the songsters an' nature's a' fadin',
An' naething can charm her whan Jonnie's awa'.

That heart maun be harder than stane without feeling,
That bosom I'm sure must be colder than snow,
When down her fair cheeks the tear drops are stealing,
That melts na at sic a true picture o' wo!

O could she ance mair but receive her sweet treasure,
The cauld blasts o' winter could gie her nae pain,
The loud roaring torrent, would add to her pleasure,
Gif she could but see her dear Jonnie again.

My Ain Fireside – By Mrs. Elizabeth Hamilton

O! I hae seen great anes, an' been in great ha's,
'Mang lords an' 'mang ladies a' cover'd wi' braws,
At feasts made for princes, wi' princes I've been,
Where the great shine o' splendor has dazzled my e'en;
But a sight sae delightfu' I trow I ne'er spied,
As the bonnie blithe blink o' my ain fireside.
Ance mair, God be thankit, by my ain heart some ingle,
Wi' the friends o' my youth, I cordially mingle,
Nae form to compel me, to feel wae or glad,
I may laugh when I'm merry, an' sigh when I'm sad;
Nae falsehood to dread, and nae malice to fear,
But truth to delight me, and friendship to cheer;
O' a' roads to happiness that ever were tried,
There's nane half sae sure as my ain fireside.
When I draw in my stool, on my cozey hearth stane,
My heart loups sae light I scarce ken't for may ain;
Past sorrows, they seem, but as dreams o' the night,
Cares flown on the winds – they're clean out o' sight.
I hear but kent voices, kent faces I see,
An mark fond affection glint saft frae ilk e'e.
Nae flickerin's o' flatt'ry, nae boastings o' pride,
'Tis heart speaks to heart at ane's ain fireside.

To The Editor
Of The Haverhill Gazette And Patriot

The following poem, sir, I send it,
In hopes your honor will befriend it;
Some Scottish bard years since had penn'd it,
  A picture true;
The theme itself must recommend it,
  Old times and new.

"RUSTIC BARD."

Poesy On An Old Tea-Pot

Ye cracked, crazy, worthless ware,
Ye're nearly done, I dinna care—
Ye've robb'd me o' ten pun' an' mair,
  Sin' first I saw ye;
Its far ayont what I can spare,
  Ill time befa' ye.

In days o' yore, lang past an' gone,
The use o' you was little known,
Nor did our ancestors think on
  This plant ca'd tea;
They had their paritch an' their sow'n,
  Ay twice a day.

But now the case is alter'd quite,
Tea maun be had baith morn an' night,
The warld's refin'd in a' men's sight –
  In a' men's view;
Naething that's ancient can be right,
  A' maun be new.

An' now that tea an' sugar dear,
Doubly advanced, or very near,
Its folly i' the extreme to hear
    O country dames,
Spending their money on sic cheer,
    They an' their weans.

Great folly i' th' extreme indeed,
For then the butter an' the bread,
Likewise the cream, I pray tak' heed,
    Stan's o' the ranks,
Or else your tea's na worth a bead,
    No wordy thanks.

An' then the time that's spent an' a'
Still adds mair speed to our down fa',
I canna bear the thoughts ava
    This mode o' life;
It ruins poor folk ane an' a'
    Man, wean, an' wife.

Our auld forebears they liv'd right weel,
On hamely fare, guid milk an' meal,
Right halesome food, for man or chiel,
    An' stout were they;
Nor pain, nor ache, did them assail,
    'Till latest day.

Then were their lives free frae excess,
Mark'd wi' content an' cheerfulness;
Nor luxuries had e'er access,
    Within their cot;
High life an' gaudiness o' dress,
    They valu'd not.

Religion too was their delight,
They sang an' pray'd baith morn an' night,
An' cordial frien'ship did unite
    Them ane an' a';
Nor envy, nor ambition's spite,
    Were known ava.

Many's religion's but a fable,
Gif they can keep a modish table,
To eat an' drink weel while they're able,
    An' mak' a show;
These are the golden rules more stable,
    By which they go.

BALLYGRANNY, *December*, 1815.

Robert Dinsmoor To The Rev. William Miltimore, Falmouth, Maine

REV. AND DEAR SIR:

I HAVE seen and read your mournful and affecting letter to your sister, N.W., announcing the death of your beloved Betsey, the dear wife of your youth, and the tender mother of your darling children – with a request to me for some of my poetry, for her grave-stone. I confess, sir, I feel myself entirely incompetent to write anything suitable to be engraven as a lasting mememto of the character of the truly worthy and amiable Mrs. Miltimore. But having prompted by a regard for the real worth and merit of the deceased, and to perpetuate the memory of one of my own acquaintance, whom I so much valued when alive, and also, from a desire to gratify you, in some measure, I wrote the enclosed epitaph, which I intended to show you, on your return from Philadelphia; at which time, I expected a visit from you, having understood you were to return through Windham. But being disappointed in my expectation, I now venture to enclose and send it to you, putting the highest confidence in your friendship and candor, trusting you will not make any undue use of it.

> Sincerely, sir, with you I sympathies,
> Your sorrow claims a tribute from my eyes;
> A debt so just, to pay it gives relief,
> "For social pleasure is in social grief."
> My heart inured to sorrow, feels for you,
> And at your tale of wo it bleeds anew!
> The clock struck twelve, when sunk in tranquil rest,
> No anxious care disturb'd the peaceful breast;
> The bold invader with his deadly spear,
> Approach'd your bed and pierced your Betsey dear!
> You saw your darling writhe, and gasp for breath,
> And close her eyes fast in the sleep of death!
> O, sir, your office long has been to try,
> And wipe the melting tear from sorrow's eye;
> Hast thou not often raging grief to calm,

With soothing words pour'f in consoling balm?
And wounded souls directed to repair,
To Gilead's balm, and the Physician there,
Where medicine alone can ease the smart,
And comfort give to every broken heart?
Your own advice—O! be not slack to try it,
The doctrine's good if wisely you apply it.

That you and your dear daughters, may experience that consolation in your trouble which the religion you profess, only can afford, is the prayer of your sincere friend.

Epitaph On Madam Miltimore*

THE week was ended, holy time begun,
Here days were finish'd, and her work was done.
The tender mother, and the virtuous wife,
Received the summons, and gave up her life!
At midnight hour, the fatal arrow sped –
On seraph wings her lovely spirit fled;
Her pious soul pursu'd the heavenly road,
To rest eternal with her Saviour, God!

Mrs. Miltimore died without any previous sickness. She awoke her husband in a convulsive spasm. He sprang and got a light, and in a few minutes she expired in his presence, a few minutes after midnight, just as the Sabbath began.

The Following Was Sent To Mr. Betton, On Returning To Him Burns's And M'Neil's Poems, Who Had Lent Them To The "Rustic Bard"

KIND friend and honorable Esquire,
Your Scottish poems I admire;
To thank you, sir, is my desire,
    Since pleas'd I feel;
Charm'd with the chord of Burns's lyre,
    And bard M'Neil.

* * * * *

But oh! the celebrated Burns,
Who sometimes for his folly mourns,
Charm'd with his sense and witty turns,
    Upon my conscience,
I think the man's a dunce who spurns,
    And calls it nonsense.

Oh! let me ne'er again engage,
To read those rhymes to J***y P*ge,
Or any other in this age,
    Of stoic art,
Lest Burns's ashes rise in rage,
    And blast me for't.

But when he paints his lovely Jean!
What beauties in the verse are seen!
Her virtuous heart can banish spleen,
    And bless his life;
My native passions rising keen,
    Adore the wife.

But now behold his aged sire!
With wife and children round the fire,
O! hear them tune the heavenly lyre,
    In martyr's air!
While love and peace each heart inspire,
    They kneel in prayer!

Would Heaven grant my highest wish,
(Though atheists mock and deists hiss,)
And of the purest earthly bliss,
    Make me partaker;
I'd form a family like this,
    And praise my Maker!

* * * * *

Then fare ye well, my loving friend,
Whose generous heart can give and lend,
With gratitude these lines I send,
    Depend upon it;
But fear your patience I'll offend,
    With my dull sonnet.

[Mr. BETTON observes that he had no pretensions to poetry, but wishing to call forth more of the native energy of the Bard, he ventured to send him the following lines in answer to the foregoing piece; and at the same time presented him with a small volume of Burns's poems.]

Answer To Robert Dinsmoor, Presenting Him With Burns, May 8, 1809

MY rhyming Rob, I got your letter,
Which, e'er I answer, I had better
My dull and drowsy muse unfetter,
  And give her play;
Perhaps she may clear up the matter
  Of my delay.

Nine moons I've had it to peruse,
Yet why should I my friend abuse?
His real goodness thus misuse?
  The muse herself.
Must, if she can, make an excuse,
  For me poor elf.

Then hear her, if you patience have,
For sure as I've a soul to save,
To me she's silent as the grave,
  When I entreat her;
To you she better shall behave,
  Or faith I'll beat her.

I ask'd her what you would expect,
For so my criminal neglect?
Quoth she, he does not care the speck
  Of his thumb nail,
Whether his thoughts you intercept,
  With your dull tale.

Quoth she, you'd time enough to spare,
To write to him, go here and there,
One reason why you did forbear,
    You live too easy;
In other words, I do declare,
    You're downright lazy.

Besides, says she, I needs must own,
That nature made you such a drone,
Ome might as well from a dry bone,
    Poetic fire
Extract, as bright as ever shone,
    As from your lyre.

Then tell friend Rob, the truth at once,
For truth will seldom give offence,
That poetry from your dull sconce,
    Can never come!
Quoth I, you'll make me out a dunce,
    Quoth she, 'tis done.

You have been striving many days,
To imitate Rob's native lays;
But let me tell you to your face,
    You can't come near;
Your head can never wear the bays,
    I'm very clear.

Quoth I, will you help me indite,
If I to him attempt to write,
In poetry this very night,
    You vile ingrate?
Quoth she, I *cherish* genius bright,
    But can't create.

I told her I could write in time,
As well as any of the nine,
And if in poetry I could not shine,
    You would forgive it;
In rhyme! quoth she – no, not a line –
    I'll ne'er believe it.

With that my patience was outdone,
My philosophy quite o'ercome;
I punish'd here for all her fun,
    And out of door,
I turn'd, and bade her never come,
    To plague me more.

And now as I have no assistance,
Of any being in existence,
My thoughts to prompt, or make assistance,
    I'll write away;
Of time it would be a mispence,
    Much more to say.

Apologies, when they're too long,
And eke a story or a song,
To me, of all things they're among
    The very dullest;
In short confessions, may belong,
    Hearts very fullest.

M'Neil and Burns are pleasing chaps,
Full of good morals, and perhaps,
Their hearts, at human frail mishaps,
    Are moved more,
Than thousands who in sordid laps,
    Do grunt and snore.

The covetous, unfeeling race
Of fellow mortals, have no place
In their cold hearts, to see a grace
    In Robert Burns;
To read, they think it a disgrace,
    "His witty turns."

But he who reads his Cotter through,
And real religion cannot view,
Is much more fitted for a stew,
    Than Zion's hill;
God grant, of such there may be few,
    And fewer still.

Look at his prayers, though they're in rhyme,
How excellent, and how sublime!
How penitent does he resign,
    To God his soul!
How to his sway does he incline,
    To yield the whole!

M'Neil in Willie Garlace shines,
His Jean gives interest to his lines,
He paints them both, in evil times,
    As well as better;
Tears have I shed for Willie's crimes,
    E'en o'er this letter.

Though I'm no poet, I can say,
I love M'Neil's and Burns's lay,
Can o'er them pore both night and day,
    And feel them both;
To lay such favorites away,
    I'm very loth.

As you love Burns, my worthy friend,
And to his beauties can attend,
His works to you I therefore send,
    Two vols. in one;
The book I give you not to lend,
    To stuttering John.

Nor yet to one of Stoic mind –
No beauties in it can he find;
And as I now feel much inclin'd
    Fast to get on,
My love to you, this must remind,
    Silas Betton.

Robert Dinsmoor To Silas Betton

MY honor'd friend, and much lov'd Silas,
Whose heart is free, and frank and guileless,
When press'd with care, the brow is smileless,
    Your lib'ral hand,
E'en pleasure, to the heart that's joyless,
    It can command.

O! how it charms my heart to read,
And see you mount your poet-steed!
Again I see you light with speed,
    The muse unhamper,
And like a lawyer finely plead,
    To make her scamper.

The sweet harmonious lines you sent me,
How to the nines, they do content me!
But yet, so high, to compliment me,
    In pathos such,
And with that glorious book present me,
    It seems too much.

My flatter'd muse I may compare,
To little Robert in a chair,
The thoughtless nurse that should take care,
    "A man," she calls;
Rob climbs again, nor thinks of fear,
    Till down he falls!

It must be deem'd gross imposition,
To set my lays in competition
With others, fam'd for erudition
    And college lore;
At least, it must be vain ambition,
    If nothing more.

No rustic modern bard can claim,
To rank so high in lists of fame;
Your song, "Tom Paul," emits a flame,
    Fair as the sun;
And shall immortalize your name,
    While rivers run.

Had I the art to make words ring,
Like lofty Burns, I'd rant and sing,
My muse should stretch her flutt'ring wing,
    And soar apace;
And flowers from off Parnassus bring,
    Your brow to grace.

Then hold your pen and "write away,"
There's no excuse for your delay;
Let loose the muse, "and give her play,"
    And never blame her;
Cast her vile fetters far away,
    Or you may lame her.

And let it ne'er again be said,
That an embargo stopp'd your trade;
Such base restrictions may be laid,
    By servile fools;
Let none e'er say that you obey'd
    Such musty rules.

Non-intercourse! the thing is hollow!
A measure causeless, vague and shallow;
The heads who form'd it sure were mellow;
    'Tis best by half,
Great Madison forthwith to follow,
    And take it off.

Believe me, sir, for all that's said,
I've no intention to upbraid,
Although your answer was delay'd,
    By your postponement;
If 'twas a crime, I'm sure you've made
    Complete atonement.

My little book, O! how I prize it;
I am afraid I idolize it;
But yet the wretch, who dares despise it,
    In proud disdain,
His sordid hands, nor stoic eyes, it
    Shall ne'er profane.

And now my worthy friend and kind,
My heart to you feels so inclin'd,
That from henceforth if you've a mind,
    Though not akin, sir,
A loving brother you shall find,
    In Robert Dinsmoor.

WINDHAM, *July* 10, 1809.

Lines Written By A Gentleman For His Wife, On A Work-Bag, With Permanent Ink

YOU request that something will write,
On what subject I'm puzzled to think;
Should it be in your praise, then I might
Use the whole of my permanent ink.

Since that hour when you gave your consent,
That your fate with my own I should link;
Our days have been mark'd with content,
Full as lasting as permanent ink.

Happy still, in life's current we sail,
For on each others' foibles we wink;
And no quicksands of passion prevail,
To stain deeper than permanent ink.

When this voyage, which with pleasure we took,
Shall be o'er, and we feel we must sink,
May our names be enroll'd in that book,
That is written with permanent ink.

By A Special Request From The Same Gentleman And His Lady, The Following Lines Were Written For The Other Side Of The Work-Bag, By The "Rustic Bard"

THY spouse must be happy, fair dame,
Whose sense doth thy virtues approve;
When you as his own he can claim,
With a heart full of permanent love.
Be thou like the true loving kind,
Or more gentle sweet cooing dove!
Then in his fond bosom you'll find,
A river of permanent love.

Your offspring around you shall grow,
Like plants in a garden or grove;
While mutual affection shall flow,
Like a fountain of permanent love.
When death brings you down as it must,
May your souls rise triumphant above;
And all your affections be lost,
In an ocean of permanent love.

To Issac M'Gaw, Esq. A Young Lawyer And His Wife, Soon After Marriage

DEAR Issac, fondly would I draw,
A summons that would stand in law;
But critics often find a flaw,
    More shrew'd than wisely;
I should have said to 'Squire McGaw,
    And wife Eliza.

But let that stand – I've more to say,
On Tuesday next, I mean to play,
Just when we've gotten in our hay;
    (If health permit;)
Come see us afternoon that day,
    And "crack and spit."

I do not wish to be mistaken,
Our best ripe apples shall be shaken;
We'll give you neither beef, nor bacon,
    Nor buck nor brock;
Perhaps we'll have a well stov'd capon,
    Or moorland cock!

No punch, nor brandy – you may risk me,
But cider in the place of whiskey;
Haply some wine, to make us frisky,
    "And what the matter?"
We will, when cheerly, talk more briskly,
    And feel the better.

No formal billet doux I've penn'd ye,
Nor flatt'ring compliment intend ye;
Please to accept the wish I send ye,
    Nor snuff, nor snarl!
And as you ever would befriend me,
    Come on your peril.

"RUSTIC BARD."

WINDHAM, *August* 23, 1823.

To Mr. Isaiah Webster, 2d, Haverhill, Mass., On The Fleeting Nature Of Time. – January 1827

TIME teaches all a serious lesion,
Its rapid course exceeds expression;
Our days and years in quick succession.
    Are past and gone;
A moment's all we've in possession,
    Nor that our own.

Should some endearing object rise,
To gratify our longing eyes,
From our embrace the phantom flies,
    A moment's pleasure;
So all our earthly comfort dies –
    Uncertain treasure!

By jarring fates, like heat and frost,
We find our expectations crost;
From thing to thing we're torn and tost,
    Of peace bereft;
Enjoyment's in privation lost,
    But grief is left.

Time carries all our joys away,
Nor can we make our minutes stay;
Those dear delights, be what they may,
    Of which we share;
Our aching hearts can only say,
    That "once they were."

Death sweeps away both great and small,
Its with'ring blast destroys us all,
Just as the leaves in autumn fall,
    So mankind must;
Heroes, and kings, and statesmen, shall
    Return to dust.

Even so the glorious Washington,
Whose deeds shine brilliant as the sun,
When he his country's freedom won,
    Resign'd his breath;
Great Adams too, and Jefferson,
    Now sleep in death.

Our first three chieftans, high renown'd,
With presidential honors crown'd;
Let patriot bards their worth resound,
    And eulogize them;
And while the wheels of time go round,
    Immortalize them.

Kingdoms and states, and empires stand,
Upheld by an Almighty hand;
Who gives them men to rule the land,
    For wo or weal;
They prosper just by his command,
    Or sorrows feel.

No bliss that's found in nature, can
Give perfect happiness to man;
His mind was form'd by Wisdom's plan,
    For joys that're higher;
He longs for things beyond his span,
    With strong desire.

Though all to us seems imperfection,
Disjointed parts without connexion,
Yet all moves on with good direction,
    And wise control;
Omniscience views with clear inspection,
    One perfect whole.

Epitaph For The Author's Wife, Who Died June 1, 1799, In The 38th Year Of Her Age

IN humble prayer, to God's kind care,
She left her babes, eleven;
And husband dear, without a tear,
And wing'd her way to heaven!

To Miss E.C.,
At The Close Of Her School, In Windham

FAIR blooming maid, instructress kind,
Long may you cultivate the mind,
   And seeds of science plant;
The native heart of ev'ry child,
Is like a forest or a wild;
   They all true knowledge want.
And when your well done task's resign'd,
Which arduous seem'd and hard;
Then may your self-approving mind,
Yield you a sweet reward!
   May blessing, increasing,
When sorrow is forgot,
   By Heaven, be given,
To crown your happy lot!

                                           "RUSTIC BARD."

WINDHAM, *September* 26, 1826.

To The Editor Of The Haverhill Gazette And Patriot

DEAR sir, when age bids me retire,
And lay aside my lute and lyre;
When all the poet's wonted fire
    Grows faint and low;
I scarce believe my works entire,
    Would raise a glow.

Nature, who doth of gifts dispose,
Talents to some at random throws,
Sometimes herself a niggard shows,
    Not flush nor free;
And genius sparingly bestows,
    On such as me.

Old age I fear will soon bereave me,
Of the small pittance nature gave me;
And now when friends in public crave me,
    I fear to show it;
Lest vanity, and pride, deceive me,
    And I should rue it.

A little volume, or collection,
With neither system nor connexion,
Produc'd by chance, without direction,
    Or studied art;
But oft the fruit of kind affection,
    Warm from the heart.

If learned critics should inspect,
Expose and laugh at each defect,
And in contempt my works reject,
    And scorn my name –
O! where's the friend that would protect,
    And guard my fame?

Since transient is this mortal state,
Death sweeps away both small and great!
I mourn my friend's untimely fate,
  Who honor paid me!
Alas! 'tis now a day too late,
  For him[18] to aid me.

A peasant bred, of humble lore,
'Twas nature taught my muse to soar;
Grant me a smile – I ask no more,
  As my reward;
Let candor spread her mantle o'er
  The "Rustic Bard."

To Rev. Mr. ———, Of B———

MY reverend friend, when lately I
Approach'd abrupt your dining room,
Your numerous offspring met my eye;
The mother fair, in beauty's bloom.

The grace was said, and all were placed
With parents' care the board around;
Politeness soon made me a guest –
Your table with abundance crown'd.

Sure 'twas a pleasing scene to me –
I shar'd the feast – no matter how,
While friendship, love, and social glee,
Sat smiling on each parent's brow!

I view'd the lovely circle round,
And thought your happiness divine!
But, something gave my heart a wound,
And said, such blessing once was mine!

Ah me! these flowers are favors lent
By Heav'n – like those who gave them birth;
And soon the father may lament
His darling mould'ring in the earth!

A silent prayer my heart respired –
Bless, O my God! the parent stock,
And as their hearts have oft desired,
Bless and preserve their filial flock!

"RUSTIC BARD."

September 11, 1827.

To Catherine Abbot,
Preceptress Of Greenland Academy

MY much respected young friend, you will be surprised at this address from me, especially at finding the enclosed paper. I must therefore explain the cause of my conduct. In our short interview, when you made a visit to my house, lately, you expressed an ardent wish that the fugitive poems of the "Rustic Bard," might be published to the world in print. And as my friend in Haverhill, that have sent out more subscription papers for that purpose, and intrusted some of them with me, I could think of no better method than to scatter them among my friends in my native state; and as you are placed as an instructress in a respectable academy, not far from your native town, my impression was, that with little trouble, you might obtain a few names among your students, or perhaps place it in the care of some of your friends, who, by your influence, would endeavor to promote the design of the thing; and when it should be thought expedient, see that it be returned to the post-master, in Haverhill, as therein directed.

ROBERT DINSMOOR.

WINDHAM, *May* 26, 1827.

To Miss Catharine Abbot

YOUNG honor'd dame, of learned fame,
    This compliment I send you –
Please to excuse, the humble muse,
    Nor let my song offend you.

Think not, dear friend, that I intend,
    Intrusion on your goodness;
I ne'er could find my heart inclin'd
    To treat the fair with rudeness.

By motives pure, I would secure,
    The ladies in my favor;
And that my lays, should meet their praise,
    I fondly would endeavour.

None can be great, in church or state,
    Except the fair allow;
Nor bard can shine, till they entwine
    The laurels round his brow!

Then, virtuous maid, grant me your aid,
    And with my rustic hand,
In some bright place, my page to grace,
    Fair Cath'rine's name shall stand.

May Heaven bestow the gift on you,
    To teach your pupils right;
And grant you grace, to fill your place
    With honor and delight.

                        "RUSTIC BARD."

To Mrs. Sarah Davidson,
The Bard's Daughter, Belfast, Maine

I.

MY Sally dear, would you be glad,
To have a line from your old dad?
Though age and wint'ry blasts pursue,
His heart still glows with love to you.
How pleasing were those hours to me,
When you were prattling round my knee!
When I did kiss, and call you sweet,
Your mother's heart rejoic'd to see't.

II.

She made your clothers, and gave you food,
And when her darlings round her stood,
She taught their infant notes to rise,
And praise their Maker in the skies!
Devotion then my soul inspir'd,
From worldly cares my heart retir'd,
And joyful did the concert join –
The song was harmony divine!

III.

Where joy like this could spring and grow,
I deem'd a paradise below!
No earthly bliss like this could be,
'Twas just a taste of heaven to me!
When I review the scenes I've past,
A gloom upon my mind is cast –
Those scenes that bless'd life's happy noon,
Alas, were all withdrawn too soon!

IV.

My life is solitary grown,
I sit and muse with ma'm alone –
I've past my three-score years and ten,
And rank with other aged men!
Yet gratitude to God I owe,
For friends and favours here below;
And when I bid them all adieu,
May Heaven's best blessings rest with you.

ROBERT DINSMOOR.

WINDHAM, *January* 17, 1828.

J.G. Whittier To The "Rustic Bard"

HEALTH to the hale auld 'Rustic Bard'
Gin ye a poet wad regard
Who deems it honor to be ca'd
    Yere rhymin' brither,
'Twould gie his muse a rich reward –
    He asks nae ither.

My muse, an inexperienced hizzie,
Wi' pride an' self-importance dizzy,
O' skills to rhyme it, free an' easy,
    Is na possessor;
But yours has been a lang time busy –
    An auld transgressor.

Yes, lang an' weel ye've held your way,
An' spite o' a' that critics say,
The memory of your rustic lay,
    Shall still be dear;
And wi' yere name to latest day,
    Be cherish'd here.

And though the cauld an' heartless sneer,
An' critics urge their wordy weir,
An' graceless scoundrels taunt an' jeer,
    E'en let them do it;
They canna mak' the muse less dear,
    To ony poet.

But why should poets "fash their thumb?"
E'en let the storms o' fortune come;
Maun they alane be left in gloom,
    To grope an' stumble;
AN' wear the garb, fate's partial loom
    Has wove maist humble?

No! up wi' pride – wha cares a feather
What fools may chance to say, or whether
They praise or spurn our rhymin' blether –
    Laud, or abuse us;
While conscience keeps within fair weather,
    An' wise men roose us.

Then let us smile when fools assail us,
To answer them will not avail us;
Contempt alane should meet the railers –
    It deals a blow,
When weapons like their ain, wad fail us,
    To cower the foe.

But whyles they need a castigation,
Shall either name, or rank, or station,
Protect them frae the flagellation,
    Sae muckle needed?
Shall vice an' crimes that "taint the nation,"
    Pass on unheeded?

No! let the muse her trumpet take,
'Till auld offenders learn to shake,
An' tremble when they hear her wake
    Her tones o' thunder;
'Till pride, and bloated ignorance quake,
    And gawkies wonder.

For ye, auld bard, though long ye're been
An actor in life's weary scene,
Wi saul erect, an' fearless mein,
    Ye've held your way;
An' O! may Heaven preserve serene,
    Your closin' day.

Farewell! the poet's hopes an' fears
May vanish frae this vale o' tears;
An' curtain'd wi' forgotten years,
    His muse may lie;
But virtue's form, unscaith'd appears –
    It canna die!

HAVERHILL, *1st month*, 1828.

Robert Dinsmoor To Edward P. Harris, Of Chesterfield

DEAR SIR, I justly am your debtor,
For your intelligent kind letter,
Advising me which way I'd better
    My books dispose of;
But evils may attend that matter,
    Which no man knows of.

Such diffidence pervades my mind,
To future prospects I am blind;
Within my little sphere confin'd,
    As if on tenters;
No part to act of any kind,
    But trust the printers.

My volume leaves, they turn and toss,
Cut out and trample on the dross –
But gold that's pure sustains no loss,
    Though tried by fire;
That they may have a brighter gloss,
    Is my desire.

Sometimes I fear – but, on reflection
They'll issue by the wise direction
Of P****, famed for deep inspection,
    And critic lore;
I think they'll have his high protection,
    And many more.

But oh! the world is large and wide,
Capricious too, and full of pride;
Both wise and simple must abide
    Its love and hate;
This is the court that must decide
    The poet's fate!

All I can tell you, more or less,
Is that the work is in the press;
But how the printer makes progress,
    I cannot say;
That he may meet with good success,
    I hope and pray.

'Tis now three months, and more, since I,
In Thayer's[19] office, chanc'd to spy,
Sheets of the bard, hung up to dry;
    Nor would he ask
Assistance, neither man nor boy –
    'Twas his own task.

By this, I think he's almost through;
And when the books are bound and new,
If there should be for me a few,
    When costs are paid,
One volume I'll reserve for you –
    But I'm afraid.

Yet, if it may your feelings suit,
And I have books to distribute,
I by these presents constitute
    No pompous pageant;
But you shall be, without dispute,
    My trusty agent.

What though some envious pedants frown,
And cry my works, as worthless down,
And hiss me as a vulgar clown,
    Say things that're hard;
Fair hands may yet with laurels, crown,
    The "Rustic Bard".

Concluding Verse For "Skip's Last Advice," Received Too Late To Be Incorporated With The Original Piece

    AE spasm caus'd a deadly grane!
    He clos'd his glimm'ring een alane,
    An' heaving neither sigh nor mane,
        In silence deep!
    Syne without sense, or seeming pain,
        He feel asleep!

CORRECTION. – In the caption to "*Skip's Last Advice,*" page first, it is said that the poem was communicated to "the Bard's *uncle*,". It should read, the Bard's *cousin*. The error was in the manuscript.

Endnotes

1. Mr. Betton was at this time High Sheriff, and had in some letter intimated that possibly he might be called, in his official capacity, to perform the duty of hangman toward the Bard.
2. Mary E. Davidson, the Bard's grand-daughter.
3. A river near Mr. Betton's.
4. Dinsmoor's spelling has been retained.
5. Z. was always known by the printers to be Mr. Betton's signature.
6. The author had almost totally lost the use of his left side, without experiencing any pain; and did not recover the use of his limbs again for some months.
7. This that Dinsmoor so much celebrated as a composer, by Robert Dinsmore, of Ireland.
8. No monument was ever erected to his memory.
9. Robert Dinsmoor, the first in America, owner of the old gun, was an emigrant from Ireland, with his family, to this country in the year 1730. He settled in that part of Londonderry now Windham, set off and incorporated in the year 1742, and by that act he was specially authorized to call the first meeting for the choice of officers, and was elected first selectman. He was one of the first commissioned officers of the Train Band, in Windham, N.H., and had the command of a party of militia, at No. 4, now Charlestown, N.H., in the time of the old French and Indian war, but exactly what date, I know not.
10. The Bard had an active part in that glorious scene.
11. This was not the first campaign they had been in the war together.
12. Fort Edward lies on the east side of the river, twelve miles above Saratoga.
13. Then called Fort Miller – the remains of the old fort were then to be seen.
14. Rev. Simon Williams.
15. The two principal leaders of the singing, in the Congregation.
16. It was erected on the same spot where a former house was consumed by fire.
17. Dinsmoor's spelling has been retained.
18. The Hon. Silas Betton.
19. Printer in Haverhill.

Glossary

For direction on how to pronounce many of the Scotch words I would refer the reader to the directions given at the head of Burns's Glossary, and in particular for the pronunciation of some of the vowells and dipthongs.

A', *all*
Aboon, *above, up*
Ae, *one*
Aff, *off*
Afore, *before*
Aft, oft, *or often*
Aiblins, *perhaps*
Ain, *own*
Airn, *iron*
Aith, *an oath*
Aits, *oats*
Alake, *alas*
Alane, *alone*
Amaist, or maist, *Almost*
Amang, *among*
An', *and, if*
Ance, *once*
Anither, *another*
Asklent, *asquint, aslant*
Athort, *athwart*
Auldfarran, or auldfarrant, *sagacious, cunning, prudent*
Auld, *old*
Ava, *at all*
Awa, *away*
Awfu', *awful*
Awnie, *bearde*
Aye, *ever, alwaysd*
Ayont, *beyond*

Ba', *ball*
Bad, *did bid*
Bairn, *a child*
Baith, *both*
Ban, *to swear*
Bane, *bone*
Bang, *beat, to strive*
Bardie, *diminutive of Bard*
Bauld, *bold*
Ben, *into the parlour*
Bethankit, *giving thanks or grace, after meat*
Beuk, *a book*
Bicker, *a short race*
Biggin, *building, a house*
Biggit, or big'd, *built*
Birk, *birch*
Blastie, *a shriveled dwarf, a term of contempt*
Blastit, *blasted*
Blate, *bashful*
Blaw, *to blow, to boast*
Bleerie, *eyes sore with rheum*
Blether, *to talk idly, nonsense*
Bletherin, *talking idly*
Blink, *a little while, to look kindly, to shine by fits*
Blude, *blood*
Bonnie, or bonney, *handsome, beautiful*

Brae, *a declivity, a precipice, the slope of a hill*
Braid, *broad*
Brak, *broke*
Braw, *fine, handsome*
Brawly, *very well, finely*
Breeks, *breeches*
Brig, *a bridge*
Brither, *a brother*
Brock, *a badger*
Brunstane, *brimstone*
Bught, *a pen for sheep*
Burdie, *diminutive of bird*
Burn, or burnie, *a water, a rivulet*
Burnie, *diminutive of burn*

Ca', *to call*
Ca'd, *called*
Caddie, *a person, young fellow*
Caff, *chaff*
Cairn, *a loose heap of stones*
Callan, *a boy*
Canna, *cannot*
Cannily, *wildly, dexterously, gently*
Canty, *cheerful, merry*
Cantraip, *a charm, a spell*
Caring, *gentle, dextrous*
Carl, *an old man*
Carlin, *a stout old woman*
Caudron, *a caldron, pot or kettle*
Cauld, *cold*
Chap, *a fellow, a blow*
Chaw'd it, *chew'd it*
Chiel, *a young fellow*
Claise or claes, *clothes*
Claith, *cloth*

Claithing, *clothing*
Claivers, *nonsense*
Clash, *an idle tale*
Cleekit, *having caught*
Clootie, *an old name for the devil*
Cood, *cud*
Coost, *did cast*
Cowp, *to tumble over*
Cowpit, *tumbled over*
Cozie, *snug*
Craik, *to converse*
Crowdie, *the proper yankee name of it is hasty-pudding*
Creepin' *creeping*
Cuif, *a blockhead, a ninny*

Daddie, *a father*
Daffin, *merriment, foolishness*
Daft, *merry, giddy, foolish*
Daur, *to dare*
Daurk, *a day's labor*
Dearie, *diminutive of dear*
Deave, *to deafen*
Deils, *devils*
Ding, *to worst, to push*
Dinna, *do not*
Donsey, *unlucky*
Dool, *sorrow, to lament, to mourn*
Douce, *sober, prudent*
Dowff, *pithless, wanting strength*
Dowie, *worn out with grief*
Downa, *cannot, am not able*
Doylt, *stupid*
Drap, *a drop, to drop*
Drappet, *dropped*

Ee, *the eye*
Een, *the eyes*
Eerie, *frighted, fear of spirits*
Eneugh, *enough*

Fa', *fall, lot to fall*
Fa's *does fall, water falls*
Fae, *a foe*
Fash, *trouble,*
Faund, or faun', *did find*
Fause, *false*
Faut, *fault*
Fearfu', *frightful*
Fear na', *fear not*
Feart, or fear'd, *frighted*
Feckfu', *large, stout*
Feckless, *puny, weak*
Ferly, *to wonder, a wonder*
Fier, *sound, healthy*
Fit, *a foot*
Fleech, *to supplicate in a flattering manner*
Fleechin', *supplicating*
Fley, *to scare*
Flickering, *to meet, to encounter with*
Flinders, *shreds, broken to pieces*
Forbye, *besides*
Forebears, *forefathers*
Forgather, *to meet, to encounter with*
Forgie, *forgive*
Fou', *full, drunk*
Fouth, *plenty, enough, or more than enough*
Frae, *from*
Frien', *friend*
Fu', *full*
Funy, *full of merriment*
Fyke, *to be in a fuss about trifles*

Gab, *the mouth, to speak boldly, or pertly*
Gae, *to go*
Gaed, *went*
Gaet, *gait, manner of walking*
Gain', *going*
Gane, *gone*
Gang, *to walk, to go*
Gar, *to force to, make*
Gart, *forced to do, compelled*
Gate, *way, road*
Gawin', *going*
Gawk, *a cuckoo, term of contempt*
Gawky, *half witted, foolish*
Gear, *riches, goods of any kind*
Geck, *to toss the head in wantonness or scorn*
Ghaist, *a ghost*
Gie, *to give, gied, gave*
Gif, *if*
Gin, *if, against*
Girn, *to grin, to twist the features*
Girnin', *grinning*
Glaurn'd, *aimed, snatched*
Glen, *dale, deep valley*
Gleg, *sharp, ready*
Glegger, *sharper, or apter,*
Gley, *a squint, to squint*
Gloamin', *the twilight*
Glower, *to stare, to look*
Glowred, *looked, stared*
Gowan, *the flower of the daisy, dandelion, &c*
Gowd, *gold*
Gowl, *to howl like a dog*
Graip, *a pronged instrument for cleaning stables*
Graith, *accoutrements, furniture, &c.*
Graith, *gear*

Greetin', *crying, weeping*
Grievin', *grieving*
Grun', *the ground*
Gude, *the Supreme Being, good*
Guid, *good*
Guidman, *master of the house*
Guidwife, *mistress of the house*
Gully, or gullie, *a large knife*

Ha', *hall*
Hae, *to have*
Haffet, *the temple, the side of the head*
Haffing, *nearly half, partly*
Hairst, *harvest*
Hale, *whole, tight, healthy*
Halesome, *healthful, wholesome*
Haly, *holy*
Hame, *home*
Han', or haun, *hand*
Happit, *hoped*
Haud, *to hold*
Hawkie, *a cow, properly one with a white face*
Hersel', *herself*
Himsel', *himself*
Hing, *to hang*
Hingin', *hanging*

I', *in*
Ilk, or ilka, *each, every*
Ingle, *fire, fire-place*
Ise, *I shall, or will*
Ither, *other, one another*

Jocteleg, *a folding-knife*

Ken, *to know*
Kend, or kent, *knew*
Kith, or kin, *kindred*
Kye, *cows*

Laddie, *diminutive of lad*
Laigh, *low*
Laith, *loath*
Lambie, *diminutive of lamb*
Lan', *land*
Land, *long*
Lane, *lone*
Lanely, *lonely*
Lap, *did leap*
Lawlan', *lowland*
Leal, *loyal, kind, faithful, true*
Lear, lore, *learning*
Lede, *to leave*
Leeze me, *a phrase of congratulation; as, I am happy in thee, or proud of thee*
Libben-knife, *gelding-knife*
Libbet, *gelded*
Lift, *sky*
Lilt, *a ballad, a tune, to sing*
Liltin', *singing*
Linkin', *tripping*
Linn, *a waterfall*
Lint, *flax*
Lison, *a precipice*
Livin', *living*
Loan, or loanin', *the place of milking*
Loanie, *diminutive of loan*
Loof, *the palm of the hand*
Loup, *jump, leap*
Lowe, *a flame*
Lowse, *to loose*
Lug, *the ear*
Lyart, *of a mixed colour, grey*

Mair, *more*
Maist, *most, almost*
Mak', *to make*
Mang, *among*
Maun, *must*
Mavis, *the thrush*
Meere, *a mare*
Men', *to mend*
Min', *mind, remembrance*
Minnie, *mother, dam*
Mirk, *dark*
Misca', *miscall, to abuse*
Mither, *a mother*
Mony, or monie, *many*
Morn, *the next day, to-morrow*
Mou', *the mouth*
Muckle, or mickle, *great, big, much*
Musie, *diminutive of muse*
Mysel', *myself*

Na', *no, not, nor*
Nae, *no, not any*
Naething, or naithing, *nothing*
Naig, *a horse*
Nane, *none*
Negleckit, *neglected*
Neuk, *nook, or corner*
Niest, *next*
Niffer, *an exchange, to barter*
Nowte, *oxen, black cattle*

O', *of*
Ony or onie, *any*
O't, *of it.*
Ourie, *shivering, drooping*
Oursel', or oursel's, *ourselves*
Ower, *over, too*

Paitrick, *a partridge*
Parritch, *oatmeal pudding*
Pauky, or pewkie, *cunning, sly*
Peisky, *a trick*
Pine, *pain, uneasiness*
Pit, *to put*
Plew, or pleugh, *a plough*
Poortith, *poverty*
Pou, *to pull*
Pout, or poud, *did pull*
Pow, *the head*
Pownie, *a little horse*
Powther, *powder*
Prief, *proof*
Prieved, *proved*
Pund, pun', *pound*

Quak, *to quake*
Quat, *to quit*

Reamin', *brimful, frothing*
Reek, *smoke*
Reekin', *smoking*
Reekit, *smoking, smoky*
Remead, *remedy*
Restruked, *restricted*
Rew, *repent*
Rief, *plenty, abounding*
Rig, *a ridge*
Rin, *to run*
Roose, *praise*
Roun', *round, about*
Routhie, *plentiful*
Routh, rowth, *enough, plenty*
Row, *to roll*
Rowt, *rolled, wrapped*
Rowte, *to low, to bellow*
Rung, *a cudgel*
Runin', *running*
Runkled, *wrinkled*

Sae, *so*
Saft, *soft*
Sair, *to serve, a sore*
Saul, *soul*
Saut, *salt [?] saut*
Scaith, *or skaith, to damage*
Scar, *to scare, to fright*
Sconner, *a loathing, to loathe*
Screed, *to tear, a rent*
Scrimp, *to scant*
Scrimpet, *scanty*
Sen', *to send*
Sel', *self, alone*
Shana, *shall not*
Shaw, *to chew*
Shaw, *a small wood in a hollow*
Shaw me, *shew me*
Shool, *a shovel*
Shoon, *shoes*
Shouther, *shoulder*
Sib, *near, akin, like a brother*
Sic, *such*
Sicker, *sure, steady*
Siller, *silver*
Simmer, *summer*
Sin, *son*
Sin', *since*
Skelp, *to strike, to slap*
Sklent, *slant*
Sklentin', *slanting*
Slaw, *slow*
Slee, *sly*
Sma', *small*
Smoor, *to smother*
Smoored, *smothered*
Snaw, *snow*
Sned, *to lop off*
Snool, *to submit tamely, to sneak*
Snowk, *to scent, to snuff like a dog*
Snowkin' roun', *smelling round*
Sonsie, *lucky, fortunate*
Souple, *flexible, swift*
Sowans, *the seeds of oatmeal sown, &c.*
Squeel, *screech, scream*
Stane, *a stone*
Stap, *stop*
Staw, *did steal, to surfeit*
Stey, *sleep*
Steek, *to shut*
Steekit, *closely shut up*
Stirk, *a cow or bull a year old*
Stown, *stolen*
Strae, *straw*
Strappan, *strapping lad, tall and handsome*
Stumpie, *diminutive of stump*
Sugh, *the continued sound of wind or water*
Swaird, *sword*
Swankie, *a light strapping young fellow, or girl*
Swap, *an exchange*
Swither, *to hesitate in choice*
Syne, *since, ago, then*

Tae, *toe*
Tak', *take*
Tap, *the top*
Tauld, *or tald, told*
Tent, *heed, caution*
Tentfu', *or tentie, heedful, cautious*
Tentweel, *take good heed*
Teugh, *tough*
Thae, *these*
Thegither, *together*
Thir, *these*
Thow, *a thaw*

GLOSSARY

Thole, *to suffer, to endure*
Thraw, *to twist*
Thrawin', *twisted*
Thud, *to make a loud noise*
Tillt, *to it*
Timmer, *timber*
Tine, *to loose*
Tint, *lost*
Tocker, *marriage portion*
Toun, *a town*
Towzie, *rough, shagged*
Trow, *to believe*
Trowth, *truth, a pretty oath*
Twa, *two*
Twad, *it would*
Twathree, *a few*
Twin, *to part*

Unkend, *unknown*
Unsicker, *unsure, unsteady*
Unskaithed, *undamaged, unhurt*
Upo', *upon*
Urchin, *a hedge-hog*
Uuco, *strange, uncouth, very great, prodigious*

Vera, *very*

Wa', *wall*
Wad, *would*
Wadna, *would not*
Wae, wo, *sorrowful*
Waes me, *alas! O the pity!*
Waifu', *wailing*
Wair, or ware, *to expend*
Wald, *chose*
Wale, *choice*

Wame, *the belly*
Wamefu', *a belly-full*
Wark, *work*
Warl, or warld, *world*
Warly, *worldly, eager on amassing wealth*
Warst, *worst*
Wat, *wet*
I wat, *I wot, I know*
Wattle, *a twig, a wand*
Waught, *draught*
Waukrife, *not apt to sleep wakerife/waukrife?*
Waur, *worst*
Wean, *a child*
Wee, *little*
Weebit, *a small piece*
Weel, *well*
Weelfare, *welfare*
Weet, *rain, wetness*
We'se, *we shall*
Wha, *who*
Whare, *where*
Whare'er, *wherever*
Whase, *whose*
Whunstane, *whinstone*
Whyles, *whiles, sometimes*
Wi', *with*
Wifie, *endearing term for wife*
Wimplin', *waving, meandering*
Win', *wind*
Winna, *will not*
Winnock, *a window*
Winsome, *hearty, vaunted, gay*
Withouten, *without*
Won, or win, *gain by conquest*
Wons, *dwells*
Woo, *to court, to make love to*
Woo', *wool*
Woody, *a rope made of withs*
Wordy, *worthy*

Wow, *an explanation of
  pleasure, or wonder*
Wrang, *wrong*
Wyle, *beguile*
Wyte, *blame*

Ye, *this pronoun is frequently
  used for thou*
Year, *is used for both singular
  and plural years*
Yerk, *a jerk*

Yestreen, *yesternight*
Yett, *a gate*
Yird, *earth*
Yont, *beyond*
Yoursel', *yourself*
Yowe, *an ewe*

Teachers' Notes

The following notes are designed for English Literature and History teachers and students who may find Dinsmoor's collection useful for a number of purposes in exploring issues related to poetry and literature; and the history of Scotland, Ireland and North America.

Language Contexts

Dinsmoor writes in a number of 'languages' in his poetry. What he terms 'Scotch' would be known today as Scots. This is part of the Germanic family of languages and it developed out of Northumbrian Old English in the early medieval period. For many centuries, Scots was a written and spoken language in Scotland and among Scottish settlers across the globe. For many people this was their everyday language that they used in the home for speaking to friends and family: but the language was also used for governmental, religious, legal, business and literary purposes. Despite certain superficial similarities to English, linguists view Scots as very much language in its own right and speakers are very proud of its long history of literary and cultural achievement.

Dinsmoor's use of Scots shows how Scottish and Scotch-Irish settlers in North America maintained their linguistic links to their ancestral homelands. Dinsmoor is keen to demonstrate his knowledge and usage of Scot's words and phrases, and his word list at the end of the book demonstrates his desire to celebrate his Scotch vocabulary as much as to make the book intelligible to non-Scots readers. His poetry also demonstrates the varieties of English language that he was capable of writing in. He displays a good grasp of polite forms of English that would have been acceptable to readers of refined poetry published in American books and newspapers. There is also strong evidence to suggest that Dinsmoor is adept in using American English in his poetry.

Given that he termed himself the 'Rustic Bard' we should assume that his poems were meant to be recited as much as they were read. A number of his poems are not in Scots, and one can discern from them a number of strong rhymes that work best with an American accent of his native New Hampshire. Ultimately, he reveals his creativity in blending the written and spoken words of his Old World and New World inheritances.

Literary Contexts

In calling himself 'The Rustic Bard' Robert Dinsmoor was alluding to the long tradition of working class, or pretend working class individuals publishing collections of poetry. In Britain, Ireland and North America throughout the eighteenth and nineteenth century dozens of men and women claimed this status in order to publicise their works. Often this helped them gain support from wealthy individuals, or as literacy levels and buying power increased among lower classes in society, provided them with a broader book buying public. Perhaps the most famous of these poets, was Robert Burns (1759–96), the Ayrshire-born Scottish poet whose work gained him worldwide popularity. Burns had the great ability of being seen as different things to different audiences. His work was interpreted by some as great radical poetry espousing freedom, international brotherhood and democracy. To others he was a patriot celebrating traditional values of nationality, religion and conservatism and to many a gifted love poet and songwriter. Dinsmoor alludes to Burns and other Scottish writer in many of poems. However, it would be unfair to say that he merely imitates him. Like other poets elsewhere excited by Burns's abilities and achievements, he enters into a conversation with him, not just borrowing his ideas and the traditional vernacular verse forms of Scotland, but developing it for an American setting and audience.

Dinsmoor's poetry offers great scope for exploring how everyday language can be used in writing poetry. His work celebrates his family, friends, community and the local natural environment. He demonstrates how effective his own vernacular mix of Scots and New Hampshire English can be to discuss profound and comic themes. Comparisons can be drawn between Dinsmoor and Burns's poetry. For example, a comparison of Dinsmoor's 'To A Sparrow' can be compared and contrasted with Burns's 'To A Mouse'. It can be argued that while both poems share many similarities, Dinsmoor is shaping his version for his own purposes and ideas. Teachers might also consider how Dinsmoor's poems can be compared to other nineteenth century and contemporary Scottish, Irish and American poets.

Historical Contexts

Dinsmoor's poetry is a useful and challenging source for students following the New England High School American History Part 1 syllabus.

The Dinsmoor family story which is chronicled in Dinsmoor's own foreword to his poems tells of his grandfather arriving from Ballymoney, Co. Antrim and immediately befriending Native Americans and being taken hostage before being released by the chief that he had befriended who believed in the concept of 'all one brother'. It fits neatly with the criteria delineated for the subject area of, 'Cultural Encounters-Europeans and Native Americans'. The role of Dinsmoor's people, the Scotch-Irish as, 'God's Frontiersmen' in both the north of Ireland and in America is humorously and accurately portrayed in the poem, 'Antiquity the Auld Gun', which echoes quite uniquely that defensive role played by these tough people in both Ireland and colonial America.

The poetry also reflects the Scotch-Irish predicament of bringing to America the language and thinking of Old Europe specifically the Scottish Doric humour and wisdom that pervades Dinsmoor's work as it does also with that other Robert the poet born just two years after Dinsmoor, namely Robert Burns. At the same time the rebel heart of the Scotch-Irish frontiersman provides a useful touchstone for anyone pursuing an examination of the prescribed topic of, 'British Colonialism'. We are told in fact that: 'Nae Dinsmoor would ere bend the knee'.

Always Dinsmoor's poetry celebrates the, 'New England Colonial Region and Culture'. Here he praises the bounty and abundance of food that grows freely and easily in his adopted homeland and there he catches the light and colours of the landscape as it then was in its naked beauty. As John Greenleaf Whittier says in comparison with Burns, Dinsmoor's concern is with the Merrimack and its crystal clarity rather than the, 'bonnie Doon' of Burns's Ayrshire.

Dinsmoor fought in the French and Indian War as did many of the citizens of Londonderry and Windham New Hampshire and when he tells us about being at Bennington and Burgoyne we get a sense of the fervour and anxiety of the American Revolution that he and many of the Scotch-Irish of New England participated in with alacrity. Here one is led to think about many of the other Scotch-Irish of New England such as General Stark and Matthew Thornton who were just two such warriors.

And so it is that Dinsmoor's poems, leaving aside their undoubted aesthetic value, provide a useful and first person observer's view of American History through the Humanities and specifically American poetry.

Dinsmoor starts with the material abundance that America offered to the settler and continues to define and to celebrate what it was to be an eighteenth and nineteenth-century Scotch-Irish American. He, like many of the Ulster Scots who settled in his locale, believed he had found, 'the Promised Land'. Knowing this it is then easy to understand why the Presbyterian divine, Rev. James McGregor who led his congregation from the banks of the River Bann in Co. Londonderry, Ireland to the banks of the Merrimack and Londonderry, New Hampshire is still often referred to as, 'The Moses of the Scotch Irish in America.'

Religious Contexts

Robert Dinsmoor was a member of the Presbyterian Church, which had originally developed as a faith after the Protestant Reformation of the sixteenth century. The theology of Presbyterianism was shaped by John Calvin (1509–64) and developed in Scotland by John Knox (c. 1513–72). In the seventeenth and eighteenth centuries Scottish and Irish emigrants brought Presbyterianism to North America, forming the first

Presbytery in Philadelphia in 1706 (a group of churches under the control of an elected court of ministers and lay members). Dinsmoor's writing would suggest that like many of his denomination he was relatively conservative, holding fast to the beliefs of his particular church and wary of alternative theological positions such as the Unitarians. While it may be something of an exaggeration to suggest his position on the 'frontier' made him more conservative in his religion, he exhibits a profound sense of the wonder and compassion of God and shares this with many individuals and communities through his poetry and letters.

Afterword

Robert Dinsmoor and his Scotch-Irish poems through the eyes of John Greenleaf Whittier

Robert Dinsmoor's poems present the reader with a unique opportunity to vicariously experience Scotch-Irish thinking and frontier life in the latter decades of the eighteenth century. The poems are set in New England but like those of his contemporary, Robert Burns, 'some are written in, the Scotch dialect'. We can go further and build a second layer of that vicarious experience by considering the impression made by the most Presbyterian of American poets on his esteemed neighbour, the Quaker poet and observer, John Greenleaf Whittier. In this respect Dinsmoor is in good company since Whittier's 'Old Portraits and Modern Sketches,' also presents comment on such luminaries as: Andrew Marvell, Placido-the slave poet, John Bunyan, Thomas Ellwood, James Nayler, Henry Wadsworth Longfellow, the Scottish Reformers and the Pilgrims of Plymouth.

Whittier proclaimed himself an enthusiast in the appreciation of Scottish poetry generally. He commented in beautifully modulated tones, 'The great charm of Scottish poetry consists in its simplicity, and genuine, unaffected sympathy of daily life. It is a home-taught, household melody.' Those last four words take readers to the heart and hearth of Scotch-Irish life and particularly to cottier child-rearing patterns of behaviour. But Whittier was not just any commentator of course, he was himself a considerable poet and thus he began to use metaphors and his words paint vivid word vignettes of everyday life in Scotch-Irish experience:

> It calls to mind the pastoral bleat on the hillsides, the kirk-bells of a summer Sabbath, the song of the lark in the sunrise, the cry of the quail in the corn-land, the low of cattle, and the blithe carol of milkmaids, "when the kye come hame" at gloaming.

It is clear that Whittier saw Dinsmoor's work as fitting within this genre of traditional Scottish rhyme which he admired for its honesty and simple unpretentious beauty:

> ... these furnish the limits of the immortal melodies of Burns, the sweet ballads of the Ettrick Shepherd and Allan Cunningham, and the rustic drama of Ramsay. It is the poetry of home, of nature, and the affections.

These admirable qualities Whittier believed to be missing from that which he termed the contemporary 'young literature' of America. He was critical of such writing as cold and overstrained, too intellectual in contrast with the straightforward emotional and loving verse in the Scottish tradition. For Whittier the world that Dinsmoor wrote about was one that celebrated Nature and the ordinary seasonal change and ceremonies of New England. He mentioned 'berry pickings' and 'sleigh rides' amongst other everyday events as being in that category. Whittier recognised Dinsmoor as the conduit that led him to this viewpoint, or as he described him 'the homespun figure of an old friend of our boyhood', and further lauded him for having 'had the good sense to discover that the poetic element existed in the simple home life of a country farmer'.

As yet in the commentary Whittier had not actually named Robert Dinsmoor but he was getting closer to doing so. He related how in looking through morning newspapers 'a few stanzas of poetry in the Scottish dialect attracted our attention'. Moreover, he soon made it clear that it was Dinsmoor's work that captured his attention. He identified the poem as, 'The Sparrow', and added ,'It has something of the simple tenderness of Burns.'

Whittier found particular lines in ,'The Sparrow' sufficiently affecting that he quoted them as they appeared in the Scots idiom:

> ... An' to the jee-side gart me veer
> An' crush thine eggs.
> ...
> Thy faithful mate flits round to guard thee.
> Connubial love! – a pattern worthy.

> ...
> What savage heart could be sae hardy
> As wound thy breast?

Whittier was obviously a student of many religious belief systems other than that of the 'inner light' philosophy, that was and remains at the core of the understanding of his own Society of Friends, consistently held from the time of its seventeenth century founder George Fox. Whittier quite correctly recognised in Dinsmoor's work the centrality of the words and cadences of the King James' Bible as being crucial to Scottish Presbyterian belief in the involvement of Divine Providence in everyday life:

> Omniscience tents wi' eyes divine
> The sparrow's fall!

Whittier then traced some historical background to enable the reader to understand where Dinsmoor was coming from in his vision of the world, or at least the New England corner of the world. He described how it was that early in the eighteenth century a considerable number of Presbyterians, 'of Scotch descent', came to America from the northern part of Ireland. Whittier also helpfully described the animosity that was harboured towards these people by the existing Old English settlers. He focussed on that when describing an incident that occurred in the Spring of 1719. He recalled the citizens of Haverhill seeing the Scotch-Irish rowing their canoes past the town. There was little sympathy when one canoe overturned in the rapids. Whittier quoted from a contemporary rustic ballad that displayed the cynical humour of the local citizens:

> They began to scream and bawl,
> As out they tumbled one and all,
> And, if the Devil had spread his net,
> He could have made a glorious haul.

Notwithstanding such unfortunate circumstances, Whittier nonetheless admired the Scotch-Irish who persevered until they arrived near Beaver Pond and knelt in prayer under a spreading oak tree at the edge of the pond and guided by their minister, Jamie McGregore they laid the foundation of settlement wherein the poet Robert Dinsmoor dwelt and where were nurtured his words to amuse and inform his fellows.

Whittier did not leave the story there but related further how McGregore's successor, who he does not name, but we know as Matthew Clark was, 'an old scarred fighter, who had signalized himself in the stout defence of Londonderry when James II and ... were thundering at its gates'.

As a final view of the tableau vivant of the Scotch-Irish in New England, the hardworking people of Dinsmoor's world creating their new Londonderry and Derry and Windham, John Greenleaf Whittier 'did proud' all concerned in the picture that these words painted:

> In a few years they had cleared large fields, built substantial stone and frame dwellings and a large and commodious meeting -house; wealth had accumulated around them, and they had everywhere the reputation of a shrewd and thriving community.

Source: John Greenleaf Whittier, *Old Portraits and Modern Sketches* (New York: Hurst, 1858), p. 266.

www.ingramcontent.com/pod-product-compliance
Lightning Source LLC
Chambersburg PA
CBHW030035100526
44590CB00011B/207